# Memorabilia Quilting

*Quilts, Clothing, Adornments*
*By Jean Wells*

C&T PUBLISHING

*To Jason, Valori, and John*

BACK COVER: "A Token of Friendship"
COLOR PHOTOGRAPHY by Ross Chandler, Bend, Oregon
BLACK AND WHITE PHOTOGRAPHY by Valori Wells, Sisters, Oregon
DECORATIVE ILLUSTRATIONS by Marina Anderson, Bend, Oregon
EDITORIAL DIRECTION by Diane Pedersen, C & T Publishing
EDITED by Candie Frankel, Jackson Heights, New York
TECHNICAL EDITING by Liz Aneloski, C & T Publishing
PRODUCTION COORDINATION, GRAPHIC DESIGN AND TYPESETTING
by Irene Morris, Morris Design
ELECTRONIC ILLUSTRATION by Virginia Coull, C & T Publishing

PUBLISHED by C & T Publishing, P.O. Box 1456, Lafayette, California 94549

ISBN: 0-914881-44-2

Library of Congress Catalog Card Number: 91-58594
Wells-Keenan, Jean.
    Memorabilia quilting : quilts, clothing, and adornments / by Jean Wells-Keenan.
        p.  cm.
    Includes bibliographical references.
    ISBN 0-914881-44-2 (pbk.)
    1. Patchwork—Patterns. 2. Appliqué—Patterns. 3. Patchwork quilts.
I. Title.
TT835.W466 1992
746.46—dc20

Printed in the United States of America
Pellon® Stitch-N-Tear® and Thermolam® are registered trademarks of Freudenberg Nonwovens, Pellon
Division. Picture This™ is a trademark of Plaid Enterprises.
Poly-Fil® is a registered trademark of Fairfield Processing Corporation.
Post-It™ is a trademark of 3M.   Rit® is a registered trademark of CPC International.
Sulky® is a registered trademark of Sulky of America®.
Tacky® and Designer Tacky® are registered trademarks of Artis, Inc.
Velcro® is a registered trademark of Velcro USA Inc.
X-Acto® is a registered trademark of Hunt Manufacturing.

# Table of Contents

# Foreword

A S I REFLECT on my friendship with Jean, I can think of no subject more fitting for her to write on than memorabilia quilting. Memories . . . our lives are so often filled with memories, and we are never quite sure when and how they will surface.

I met Jean at a quilting conference in 1982, and we immediately became friends. I have visited her in Sisters, Oregon, and have met her family. I was impressed by the wonderful relationship Jean has with her husband and children and how she relies on them for advice and encouragement. Jean is a very giving person and openly shares her ideas with colleagues and friends. She is never afraid to ask for advice. It is such a pleasure to spend time with Jean, and I find her ideas, her work, and her surroundings very inspiring.

Jean and I are often mistaken for sisters. Several years into our friendship, we were surprised to discover that not only were we the same age but we were born one month apart at the same hospital in California. It also happened that our fathers were both flight instructors at the military base, though they did not know one another.

Jean's caring, sensitive manner, combined with her extraordinary creative talent, brings special meaning and personal flair to her work. Antique laces, colorful ribbons, decorative buttons, collector beads, and family findings are among the tools of the trade that she so cleverly intertwines into the body of her work. She shares here a unique style that transcends identification with a specific time period, reaching instead for a timeless quality that will satisfy the yearnings of generations to come. Every quilt, each piece of clothing, the smallest adornment radiates a warm, comfortable feeling, attractively designed in a signature that is decidedly Jean's.

—DONNA WILDER,
*Director of Marketing, Fairfield Processing Corporation*

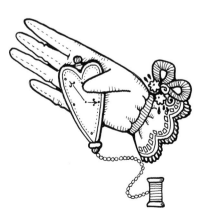

# Acknowledgments

MANY PEOPLE INFLUENCE one's writing and producing of a book. I wish to say thank you to Carolie and Tom Hensley for believing in my writing and creative abilities; to Todd and Tony Hensley for their never-ending energy, insight, and support; and to Diane Pedersen for her patient and capable attention to details.

Thank you to Candie Frankel, whose careful and thoughtful editing ensured that the words, drawings, and text would flow as they do; to Liz Aneloski, who checked and double-checked the project directions; to Marina Anderson, who managed to capture the essence of sewing with memorabilia in her illustrations; and to Irene Morris, who designed each page and brought the book to life.

Thank you to Cherie Ferguson and Sharon Thenell for handling the finishing work on some of my projects; to Valori Wells and Dennee DeKay for their enthusiastic photo styling and modeling; to Lindsay Warner, Brittany Reed, and Alyssa Boley for modeling the children's clothing; to Mary Jahns and Ursula Searles for their quilting; and to Cathi Greenberg, Carrol Clark, and Aunt June for their inspiration and friendship.

Thank you to my students throughout the years, from my first junior high boys and girls to the quilters I teach today—you continue to inspire me. Quilting friendships are enduring; they sustain me in times when other friendships do not. For me, there is something magical about helping people tap their creativity. An energy seems to flow in the process of learning, and ideas are generated in the exchange as we move from one level to another.

Thank you to my parents and also to my grandparents, who lived close by as I was growing up and whose presence greatly influenced my life. When I was a little girl, my grandfather used to say to me, "Jeannie, you can be anything you want to be!" I believed that I really could reach for the stars, so to speak. I feel very fortunate to look back on quiet times on the Metolius River, sitting on the riverbank with Grandma Tot. Both of my grandmothers were talented with the needle and spent long hours with me giving of themselves. Life's experiences create the foundation for memorabilia quilting.

Thank you to my son, Jason, for his quiet presence and straight, objective outlook on design, color, and life in general. I can always depend on him for insight. Last year he gave me an antique double wedding ring quilt for my birthday. I was touched that he would buy me a quilt and surprised at how much he knew about it. He had been listening and observing in his twenty-two years more than I realized.

Thank you to my daughter, Valori, for her artistic contributions and encouragement. She has a real "eye for design," and her touch with photographic styling is an art. I appreciate her honest comments when I struggle with an idea. When Valori was five years old, she used to come to my store, The Stitchin' Post, after kindergarten. One day I was helping Peggy, a customer and friend, pick out trim for a child's dress. The telephone rang and I went to answer it. When I looked back, Valori had taken over and was suggesting trims.

Thank you, finally, to my husband John, whose never-ending patience and understanding of my drive and intensity have seen me through many a deadline.

# Reflections— An Introduction

 FEW YEARS AGO, I found myself with pneumonia. Confined to bed (doctor's orders) and bored to tears, I snuck down to my sewing room, gathered up all the magazines I hadn't had time to read, and grabbed a pad and pencil. Even though my body needed rest, my mind was racing with ideas.

*Memorabilia Quilting* was conceived at that time. Today, three years later, you hold the result of that day's musings in your hands.

I had been toying with the idea of documenting my style of fabric ornamentation for some time. I wanted to write a book with a timeless quality, one that could be used as a reference for years to come. In my first book, *Patchworthy Apparel,* I showed my grandmother's laces on a vest. This vest was the beginning for me. Sewing the good parts of damaged or torn lace to a garment felt so "right." I found my energies and senses responding to the many textures and designs found in laces, buttons, and ribbons. Before long, these adornments traveled to my quilt surfaces, and they have been my signature ever since.

It is the use of such adornments and found objects, rather than bold or contrasting color, that gives memorabilia quilts their "sparkle." I use accent stitching to enhance the shapes and call attention to the detailing. Working the finishing details and adding all the extra touches is my favorite part of the creative process. Many of my quilts you could call "intimate" quilts—to be truly appreciated, they must be viewed up close. The smaller quilts can be hung with other objects in a grouping. I think there is a place in the quilting world for this style of treasure.

Memorabilia quilts show off the interests and personal histories of their makers right on the quilt surface. The collection of adornments is highly individual, and each item means something special. My collections tend to have a soft, elegant mood to them. They speak of quiet times, pretty things, a love of flowers and the out-of-doors. Traditional quilts are the foundation of my work, and I spring off them to create designs for today. I like to play with traditional elements, rearranging them in a way that enhances the present.

In memorabilia quilting, every stitch I take intertwines memories of my sewing past with the present. When I was nine, I designed clothes for my dolls, crudely cutting whatever fabric I could find and stitching the seams by hand or on the sewing machine. Each year at Christmastime, my grandmother sewed a new wardrobe for my favorite doll. Her sewing was much admired by me then, and I am still in awe today of the little pointed collars, rabbit fur-trimmed cape, and formals—all with tiny stitches—that grandma was able to fashion. Grandma's fingers must have been smaller than mine and her talent greater to have been able to create the things she did.

Just as my grandmother stitched memories for me, I find myself doing the same for my children. Creating a wardrobe for Valori's dolls or sewing the prom dress she designed, piecing a bear's paw quilt for Jason, stuffing his bear Sam, or making his "Celebrate America" quilt—projects like these have a special place in my heart. Stitching is a way to connect with my children, to create memories for myself as well as for my family and friends.

Before beginning your first project, read chapters 1–6 (they are arranged as if you were attending my classes) and browse through the photographs for an overall picture of memorabilia quilting. Memorabilia quilts are one-of-a-kind creations. While I will give you all the help and encouragement I can in the way of questions to ask yourself and guidelines in designing, you must make the key decisions about the direction of your project.

Basic quilt blocks and quilting techniques that are already familiar to you will be the foundation for your individual designs. But you will find yourself making new decisions beyond just what color fabric to put where. When you work with your collection, you may have to devise a way to attach it to the quilt surface or you may need to redraft a quilt block to fit a particular idea in the quilt design. I have always delighted in finding solutions—"creating responses"—to stitching and design problems, and I hope you will too. Dealing with quilting dilemmas hands-on has helped me develop techniques that are timesaving as well as effective.

Let the many personal designs and tips in this book be the inspirational starting point for your own creations. They will help you come up with ideas of your own and suggest ways to carry them out.  Above all, let your collection speak to you. Trust me! Given time to think and ponder, you will find the right path to follow for your memorabilia quilting projects. Half the fun is collecting the fabric and findings and formulating the ideas. Treasure the time spent in the process.

I hope *Memorabilia Quilting* helps you create memories from the past for years to come.

# CHAPTER ONE

# Capturing the Mystique of Memories

T HERE IS A CERTAIN MYSTIQUE to capturing memories in a quilt. Memories are yours; you "own" them. Your collection will seldom have the same impact on another person unless you are intimately acquainted and share some of the same experiences. Even so, your memorabilia quilts can still be thoroughly enjoyed by others. "A Token of Friendship" (back cover) symbolizes friendship to me and reminds me of people and events in my life. But someone else might enjoy it purely for the variety of gloves and the use of ribbons, buttons, and laces as embellishments. The mystique for the maker comes in being able to capture the memories on the quilt surface. The mystique for the viewer is generally not sentimental interest but curiosity about how unusual items are unexpectedly combined. The viewer wonders, "How would that look on my quilt surface?"

Memorabilia quilting always involves an emotional journey. "Celebrate America" (photo 13) will forever remind me of the uncertainty I felt about my son being at war, the swelling of pride I felt, in turn, that he was able to serve his country, and, finally, the tremendous relief when he returned home. Sewing and quilting had provided an outlet for me for years, and when I turned to quiltmaking during this disturbing time in my life, it was like falling into the arms of an old friend. Sewing this quilt helped me work through my many emotions during the war; today, the finished quilt has its place in the history of our family as well as of our nation. Memories sewn into a quilt can help you remember and relive the people, places, and events in your life, and they afford other viewers a similar window on part of your journey.

Memories come in all forms. In "Cows, Cows, and Moo Cows" (photo 11), cow enthusiast June Jaeger used red, black, and white cow fabrics with a blue accent to set the color scheme. A cow greeting card is stitched into a block, a ceramic cow with sunglasses is pinned to another block, and the prairie points have cow fabric fused inside. June loves cow memorabilia of all kinds, and this quilt makes her laugh whenever she looks at it. The quilt surface offered her the opportunity to display part of her collection.

When I was a little girl, my grandmother ran a drugstore. I can remember her giving me a set of paper dolls from the store one day when I was there. At the time, I was kind of disappointed because they were "old." Through the years, I kept those paper dolls, and today I am thrilled to have them. My framed collage (photo 17) uses them and also incorporates laces that belonged to that same grandmother. I will pass this treasure to a grandchild someday with a written history attached to the back. Creating and preserving memories like this helps us hold onto our roots as we move into the future.

> SIGN YOUR QUILTS. DOCUMENT IMPORTANT FACTS ABOUT THE QUILT OR THE TIME FRAME WHEN IT WAS MADE. TODAY'S QUILTS ARE CREATING MEMORIES FOR FUTURE GENERATIONS.

Deciding on a theme for your project is easy when you start with memories. Any type of memorabilia is fair game: Mementos from a daughter's ballet career, a son's senior year, family travels—even favorite hankies from grandma—will set your mind into motion. Sometimes pictorial fabrics, a collection of gloves or keys, or tickets or tokens from some special occasion will spark an idea. Gather up a collection of related items and adornments, such as ribbons, cards, pins, and buttons, that might enhance the collection. Once an idea takes hold, start thinking how to carry it through in terms of colors and fabrics. Keep collecting!

When I started "A Token of Friendship" (back cover), I wanted to capture moments of friendship and sharing. I've always loved heart and hand themes, and I hit on gloves as the perfect extension of hands. (They were easy to appliqué too!) Some of the gloves were mine years ago, one pair Valori wore at eighth grade graduation, the silver glove is from a trip to New York, and others were given to me.

The glove idea in motion, I began jotting down notes about friendships and made lists of items that might work on the quilt. The hardest part for me was working out the colors. I wanted an old-fashioned, Victorian theme with dark reds and blacks, but as I began working on the quilt, I discovered that my dark reds and blacks were too close in value. Viewed from just three feet away, the colors almost became one. So back to my fabric collection I went. This time I pulled floral fabric on a black background. I began to visualize how curvy lines in the floral designs would create movement in the quilt. They suggested femininity . . . softness . . . prettiness to me. This mood seemed to fit well with the gloves. Once I had the new fabrics with their wider color range spread before me, it was evident that the blacks and reds were too limiting a palette, but I didn't see that earlier.

Memorabilia quilts often present challenging design and construction problems. As I proceeded with "A Token of Friendship," I matched gloves with fabrics, working a layout for each block. But because no two gloves were exactly alike, the finished block size was difficult to determine. Still, settling on a block size was critical to giving the quilt continuity. I came up with two approximate sizes that could fit horizontally or vertically. To carry through my theme of old-fashioned affection and friendship, I hand-stitched everything in place.

As I sewed, I thought ahead about how I might use the adornments I had collected. Ribbons, laces, buttons, and other trinkets are special to me; they help enhance a theme. For "A Token of Friendship," I constructed an envelope from fabric, found a place for a pretty handkerchief and some antique sewing tools, and put together a ribbon nosegay for Valori's graduation gloves.

As I continued to sew gloves and laces to their respective fabrics, ideas bubbled inside me. Next came an inspiration for a border. For an antique look, I decided to piece satin fabric in the log cabin "courthouse steps" arrangement. Nontraditional fabrics like satins add a sparkle when used with cottons. The scalloping idea for the second border was suggested by the curvy floral prints of the interior fabrics.

Once the border sizes were determined, I got out graph paper and adjusted the interior block sizes to correspond with the border repeats. A few empty spaces resulted, which I was able to fill with repeat designs to further embellish the quilt. I call these fillers "stretcher strips."

At this point, you are probably asking why I didn't just start on graph paper. Sometimes I do when I have more of a plan in mind. But generally, I experiment with fabric first. Remember that memorabilia quilts are unlike other quilts because of the collected pieces that want to find a home on the surface. More trial and error is involved in planning. The individual elements of this quilt needed to fall into place before I could visualize it enough to put it down on paper. Once an idea starts to gel, get out the graph paper and draw a plan. In "A Token of Friendship," I never dreamed that the border decisions would determine the final block size.

By sharing the process involved in creating "A Token of Friendship," I hope to convey a method of working that can create beautiful solutions for you. Whenever you embark on the creative process, be aware that it is just that—a process. Be patient with yourself and give an idea the time that it needs. Keep in mind that decisions eventually make themselves. When you allow time for impressions and solutions deep within you to come to the surface, you add to your quilt's mystique.

I now know that no matter how stumped I feel, eventually an idea will come to me that is perfect for a particular quilt. "A Token of Friendship" was in process for six months, then took its final form in one week. I have become more patient as I wait for solutions to suggest themselves, and I keep enough projects going, as I am sure you do too, so I freely flow from one to another.

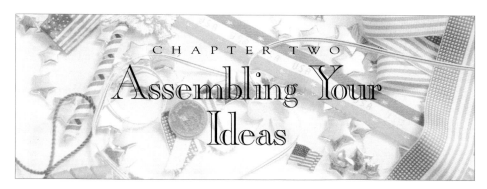

# CHAPTER TWO

# Assembling Your Ideas

 PLANNING IS IMPORTANT in quilt design, but I find that in memorabilia quilting the plan needs to be flexible. The collection dictates so much of the designing. Scales of blocks change, stretcher strips are sometimes necessary, and you need to be open to fresh inspirations. Once an overall plan is in motion, decisions seem to make themselves.

The planning process will vary depending on whether you are making quilts, clothing, or adornments. The parameters below focus on characteristics special to each group of projects. Remember that my suggestions are guidelines; rely on your instinct.

## QUILTS

### ❦ Sizing Up Your Collection

Begin planning your quilt by studying your collection of memorabilia. Place the items on a large work surface to see what kind of space they need to be displayed. Move things around to get a feel for what pieces might work together and which ones need to stand alone. A collection may lead to a technique as simple as working a few pieces of Battenberg lace into the surface ("Evening Sky," photo 37). Let the nature and size of the collection determine the scale of the quilt. A collection of buttons needs a smaller format than a collection of gloves.

**The center of interest.** Think of the collection as the "center of interest." All aspects of the design should point to the collection and help it stand out. The sizes of the pieces in the collection will determine the size of the blocks. You don't want small or delicate items lost on too large a block. "Carolyn's Keys" (photo 30) shows a Sunbonnet Sue in jail that's just the right scale for the key ring. A simple format is usually best since a collection can appear busy.

Jot down various parameters as they come to you—approximate size, arrangement of the collection, color palette, theme. Ask yourself questions: Will pieced blocks or appliqués be used in the design? Will the quilt be framed? Hung on a dowel? Put on a bed? Even when you plan ahead, surprises can pop up. "Carolyn's Keys" ended up very heavy with all the keys sewn on and had to be framed. Marrell wasn't expecting that in the beginning.

**What shape is it?** Don't be surprised if your collection leads to a nontraditional quilt shape. "Celebrate America" (photo 13) is an example. Though the interior area is kind of blocky, more graceful lines developed above and below, and it only seemed natural to make the three-tiered top and point at the bottom.

> MEMORABILIA QUILTS ARE UNLIKE OTHER QUILTS BECAUSE THE COLLECTED PIECES WANT TO FIND A HOME ON THE SURFACE. MORE TRIAL AND ERROR IS INVOLVED IN PLANNING.

## Making Sense of Your Collection

1. *Do the items need to be grouped or should they stand alone in separate blocks?*

2. *Is a block repeat the best backdrop or might a collage approach be better? "Four-Block Sampler" (photo 29) uses four basic blocks. Each one is repeated diagonally across the quilt. "Fantasy Basket" (photo 7) puts different ribbon adornments on each block. "A Token of Frienship" (back cover) uses the block collage approach.*

3. *Could the items become a border? "Hanky Memories" (photo 15) uses hankies appliquéd in crazypatch fashion for the border. This effective border displays the hankies while lending continuity to the quilt.*

4. *Do the individual items need framing? Attic window is a great framing block. "Heart Button Collection" (photo 31) is framed in the attic window technique.*

**Using a grid**. Working within a grid can simplify the design process. For instance, a 12" grid can be divided by 6, 4, 3, and 2 to create smaller elements. By relying on a grid, you can design blocks of different sizes that will all fit together easily. "Cows, Cows, and Moo Cows" (photo 11) is based on a 4" grid.

### The Fabric Palette

Choose a palette of fabrics to enhance or showcase the collection. If you are drawn to a print, make sure that the mood of the print reflects the theme of the collection and doesn't compete for attention. For sparkle, look no further than the collection itself. Its texture will stand out against the fabric background. Or you can work a nontraditional fabric, such as velvet, satin, or moiré, into your design as the sparkle.

**Challenges**. Challenges keep me on my toes and help my mind grow in new directions. Challenges come in different forms—some are "built in" as part of the job and others I take on just for fun. Maybe you have a limited fabric palette or the finished quilt must be a certain size. Perhaps the quilt is a commission and calls for colors that are hard for you to work with. I ask students to make sure that they have one or two challenges each time they begin a project. Challenges set you up to solve a problem and learn from it.

### Repetition

It's important to tie together the ideas in your quilt by repeating themes, shapes, and colors. In a traditional quilt, a single block is repeated many times over for continuity. In memorabilia quilts, the repetition can take other forms.

"A Portrait of Hearts" (photo 36) repeats both shape and color. Heart appliqués of many different sizes are unified by a single large heart in the center of the quilt. The modified heart shape of the entire quilt echoes the design. An all-white color scheme helps produce a soft, intimate mood. Subtle changes in texture are created by hankies, ribbons, buttons, and satin, moiré, and linen fabrics—all of them white.

Repetition will give any quilt unity! Take a few moments to look at the quilt photographs in the color section and jot down ideas that you like, ones that might work for you.

# CLOTHING

Clothing has always provided an outlet for my creative ideas. When my children were younger, I used their clothing to create fantasies. A little girl's size 4 dress is still my favorite format; the proportions are just perfect for design. Clothing projects take less time to complete than most quilts. It is fun to wear—or see others in—something that you have created.

## ❦ Ensemble Making

I like to envision a patchwork garment as part of an entire ensemble as I am designing it. If I am sewing a vest, I want to know what skirt, pants, or dress will be worn with it. More often than not, I buy a skirt first and then design a vest to match. The button-adorned vest (photo 1) was the result of a blouse purchase. I fell in love with the brass buttons on the blouse collar, and as I drove home from the store, my mind started racing with ideas for a vest. Think in terms of the whole outfit, and you will avoid making garments that look like "afterthoughts."

Patchwork garments also affect the look of your ensemble. A quiet backdrop can make a patchwork piece stand out, whereas a print backdrop will help it blend in. A simple black dress, for instance, can help show off a dramatic pieced vest. Decide what look you want to create, and browse through fashion magazines for ideas. Remember, you are the creator, and you control how it is going to look.

## ❦ Feeling Comfortable

**Wearability**. I like to be able to really wear the garments I make—to make sure the clothes I design fit the activities of my daily life. For me, that translates to less color contrast, but you may like a brighter, more exotic look. It has taken me years to be able to create a garment for the Fairfield Fashion Show and not be concerned about where it will be worn. No matter how hard I try, my practical side makes sure my garments are wearable!

This reminds me of an incident that occurred several years ago. My son went with me to a class, since I had to drive over the mountain and it was snowing heavily. He quietly read a book while I taught for the day. Several weeks later, I was working on a jacket and couldn't decide if I liked the sleeve or not. I asked my children what they thought, and Jason surprised me by offering the same advice he had heard me give my class. "Well, mom," he said, "can you wear it with your nonquilting friends?" Ever since then, I have never forgotten to ask myself that simple little question. It's the ultimate test.

**Your figure.** My other pet peeve is that a garment should flatter the body. Very few of us have what I would call a perfect figure. As a designer, you have an opportunity to choose colors and lines that are flattering to you. You can create a slimmer look, add the illusion of body weight, or hide a figure flaw. Make those opportunities work for you. Since a patchwork garment is going to attract attention, make sure that you attract attention where you want to.

## Clothing Designer's Quiz

1. *How will you use contrast? Will you use changes in color, texture, or embellishments? Will the contrast occur within the garment, or will the entire garment contrast with the rest of the ensemble?*

2. *Does the direction created in the piecing carry the eye in the direction you desire?*

3. *What is the underlying theme? Casual? Elegant? Country? Victorian? The design shapes and materials should speak to the theme.*

4. *Are you planning to piece on a foundation? Flannel or muslin is more drapable than batting and cooler in warm climates.*

5. *Can you wear your finished garment with your nonquilting friends?*

## ❦ Three-Dimensional Design

I use commercial patterns for my garments, making simple adjustments. Look for patterns that are simple in nature and have an area where piecing or appliqué can be shown off. Visualizing the finished three-dimensional garment is very important. Lay your paper pattern flat on a table and examine it. Keep in mind that those last three or four inches going toward the side seam will fall on the side, not the front, of your body. You'll also "lose" a few inches at the shoulder seams. In fact, the entire pattern will appear wider lying flat than it will on your body.

Now that you have narrowed down the design area to those parts that are really going to show, you will find it isn't very large. Plan your fabric layout so the important part of the print falls in the center, not under your arm. Keep the piecing simple as you near the neckline dip and the armseye.

**Adjusting commercial patterns**. Figure 2.1 shows how to make simple adjustments to a vest. As long as you keep the interior shape the same on a vest, you can change the neckline and bottom edge. Certain types of piecing work better on styles with points. Strip piecing, for instance, can be trimmed to fit a pattern without distorting the design. You can adjust skirts on dresses as long as the bodice remains intact. Sleeves can be made fuller by slitting them and pushing them apart (figure 2.2), or smaller by slitting and overlapping.

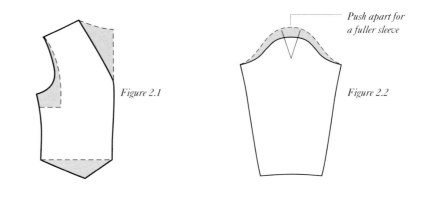

*Figure 2.1*

Push apart for a fuller sleeve

*Figure 2.2*

## ADORNMENTS

Small projects like belts, pins, screens, and pillows work up fast and provide opportunities to try out colors and techniques before you commit to a larger-scale project. I have always liked making small items for gifts. Because the entire project is smaller, piecing needs to be scaled down and the decoration made more intimate. When I make button jewelry, I decide first on the size of the piece, then I gather buttons and a few ribbons. The ribbons, while secondary in the design, help bind all the pieces together.

Screens are a little larger in scale and require a different approach. I determine the size of the screen according to its function. If I'm making one for photographs, I will lay some photos out on my gridded cutting mat, which helps me to plot the size. Once the size is determined, I can choose the materials and trims. Most of the time, some decorative trim is used. I like things to have a finished look, so I pay close attention to details.

Pillows fall in the realm of small quilts but still need to be treated separately. A pillow is stuffed and thus takes on a three-dimensional shape. Keep that shape in mind and emphasize the design toward the center where it will show.

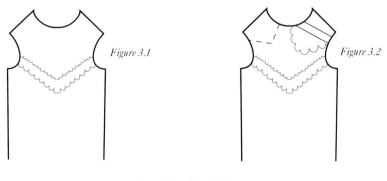

# CHAPTER THREE

# Interplay of Laces and Linens

ANTIQUE LACES AND LINENS have always intrigued me. Both of my grandmothers made lace and edgings, and as a child I watched them crochet. Feelings of nostalgia come over me when I pick up some precious piece of handmade lace. I wonder who made it and what she was like. Giving these laces and linens a home in my garments and quilts lets me preserve something of the past.

The scalloped and fluted edgings of laces not only appeal to me, the shapes often suggest a quilting design. Round, oval, and square doilies and antimacassars can be combined in my layered appliqué designs. Flat lace yardage and small crocheted motifs can adorn quilts, pillows, and hearts.

## LAYERED APPLIQUÉ

Layered appliqué can be used on any surface where you want a collage look. It might be a dress yoke, a collar, or a pillow top.

The white-on-white blouse (photo 4) uses new hankies, Battenberg laces, and doilies, all readily available. A purchased denim jacket (photos 20 and 21) is trimmed with a floral chintz fabric, Battenberg lace, pearls, roses, ribbons, and rhinestones. Antique laces are used for the little girl's dress bodice (photo 10) and collar (photo 8). Napkins, dresser scarfs, and the corners of old linen tablecloths are also good finds for this type of project. Garments with a touch of old lace are classic and timeless in nature and have an updated Victorian look.

The patterns in the pieces you collect will influence the final design that evolves. Look at your laces for inspiration. The instructions below are general in nature and offer a starting point for your own design. You will need to adapt them to your particular project.

*Figure 3.1*

*Figure 3.2*

*Layered Appliqué Collage*

## Layered Appliqué...

### ON A GARMENT:

1. *Choose the area of the garment to be appliquéd. On a shirt or blouse, determine how far down the design should appear. (It would be difficult to tuck in an appliquéd design.)*

2. *If you are sewing the garment from a pattern, stitch any necessary seams, such as the shoulder seams on a blouse, dress, or jacket.*

3. *Begin with the placement of the lowest pieces, nearest the bottom of the garment, and layer upward (figure 3.1). Pin in place. As you add new laces, trim away any excess bulk underneath. You are preparing the layers for top-stitching, one onto another (figure 3.2).*

4. *While you are layering, think about whether you want to add ribbons, buttons, cordings, or trims (photo 21) or use laces only (photo 4). Add any extra embellishments now, tucking in loose ends and pinning in place.*

5. *Topstitch with monofilament thread or handstitch with sewing thread. Sew through all layers, being sure to anchor any loose trim ends as you go.*

6. *Add quilting as a final touch in the open spaces if you wish (photo 9). Ribbon, buttons, trims, and "echo" quilting can enhance the design.*

### ON A PILLOW, QUILT, OR OTHER FLAT SURFACE:

*Follow the instructions above, but begin layering in the center. Work around, covering the surface, until you reach the outer edges. All other steps remain the same.*

## Assembling a Collage

1. Cut cardboard backing and batting to fit the frame you have chosen.
2. Layer the cardboard, batting, and collage background fabric on a flat surface. Place the frame on top. This defines the design area.
3. Begin arranging the major items of the collection in the frame. You can start at a corner and move down, or you can make the center a focal point and work out.
4. Once the main items are placed, decide what supporting items are needed to tie the collection together. Remember that the supporting items should enhance and repeat the theme but not compete with the main focus. Most of the time, you will find yourself eliminating some of your collection.
5. Fine-tune the placement. For interest, let items overlap and fade into the edge of the frame.
6. Once everything is in place, stitch or glue down. If something is extra special to me, such as the paper dolls from my grandmother, I sew it down just in case I want to remove it later on.
7. Pull the edges of the fabric around the edge of the cardboard and glue it to the back (see screen instructions, figure 7.61). Place the piece in the frame.
8. Continue the collage by decorating the frame. French silk ribbon with wired edges is great for frames because it crinkles and can be molded into different shapes (photo 17). You could also add a nosegay to the top of the frame (photo 18).

## COLLAGES

Anytime you combine several different items on a surface, you are creating a collage. The two framed collages (photos 17 and 18) show the possibilities of this technique. You start with a collection and gather "connectors"—narrow ribbon, little flowers, pieces of lace—to help tie the major items together. If you have a frame picked out when you begin, you can use it as you arrange the collection to visualize the finished piece.

## QUILTED LACE MAKING

I have been intrigued by the quilted lace concept ever since I saw Miranda Stewart's beautiful shawl made for the 1990 Fairfield Fashion Show. It looks like Battenberg lace from a distance. Miranda gave me a lesson in her lace-making technique and permission to share it with you.

A few simple quilted lace designs are shown in the patterns on pages 90–91. From these designs, the child and adult collars and handbag (photos 2 and 3) were made. Quilted lace has a cutout look to it that resembles Battenberg lace, except all the sewing is done by machine. Two layers of cotton fabric have a flat, dense batting (Miranda Stewart used Poly-Fil Cotton Classic) sandwiched in between. This batting helps keep the piece flat after stitching. The design edges are satin-stitched.

## To Make Quilted Lace

1. Study one of the patterns (pages 90–91). You will see that the flowers are joined by tiny bars. Depending on what shape you want the finished lace, the flowers and leaves can be repositioned to shape around a neck or flow down the front of a dress. Just remember when adapting a pattern to connect the flowers with the tiny bars so all sections remain attached.
2. Trace the desired design on paper and cut it out. Transfer the design onto white cotton fabric (top). Transfer the veins on the leaves and the detailing on the flowers.
3. Layer the marked fabric and backing with a flat, dense batting in between. Hand-baste with long stitches.
4. Zigzag (do not satin-stitch) around all of the shapes.
5. Using small, sharp embroidery scissors, cut out the excess fabric and batting in the background and around the edge of the design. Cut close to the stitching.
6. By machine, satin-stitch the design. Sulky rayon thread fills in nicely on satin stitch. If you have trouble satin-stitching, put Pellon Stitch-N-Tear, a stabilizer that looks like interfacing, underneath the layers to be appliquéd.
7. To create a dimensional effect, mark and cut out a second leaf. Satin-stitch around the edge, then place it on top of an existing leaf and sew down the middle through all layers to attach it.
8. Embellish the centers of the flowers with plain and covered buttons and circle ribbon flowers.

# CHAPTER FOUR

# Ribbon Renaissance

 ibbons come in a variety of textures, widths, and colors—I love working with all of them. They started cropping up in my garments eleven years ago, and now they have crept into my quilt designs. The change in texture and added quality of adornment truly enhance a project.

Working with ribbons is a creative process in itself. About ten years ago, I started doing free-lance work for Offray Ribbons. Offray would send me a palette of ribbons, and my job was to create a garment or accessory that featured the ribbons as the focus and could be used as a marketing tool. The opportunities provided by this work helped me to become more creative. Because I use ribbons freely in my quilting designs, people associate me with ribbon techniques.

"Fantasy Basket" (photo 7) is a quilt sampler of ribbon techniques you might like to try. By itself, ribbon is a flat, woven trim, but there's a lot you can do with it! Satin will easily turn and form a loop. The stiffer grosgrain ribbons have a mind of their own. The new French silk ribbons have thin wire concealed in the edges—they can crinkle and twist and hold their shape in ways that traditional ribbons cannot. Many times, the ribbon effect you envision doesn't happen on the first try and you must keep experimenting until you devise a method that works.

Many of the ribbon techniques detailed here are outgrowths of my experiments. As you study them, I would suggest that you make yourself a little sampler that you can tuck in with your experimental quilting projects. Refer to the sampler when you need to refresh your memory. By actually trying these ribbon techniques, you will think of ideas on your own. The key is in doing it.

WHEN AN IDEA HITS, I LIKE TO TRY IT AS SOON AS POSSIBLE SO THAT I CAN SEE IF IT WILL ENHANCE THE QUILT. IF I DON'T TRY THE IDEA FAIRLY SOON, IT HAUNTS ME UNTIL I DO.

# Basic Ribbon Techniques

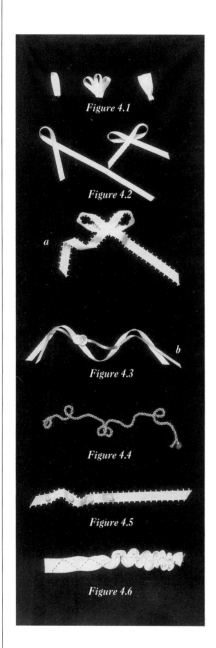

Figure 4.1

Figure 4.2

Figure 4.3

Figure 4.4

Figure 4.5

Figure 4.6

*The yardage needed for each technique will vary, depending on the width of ribbon used; a ⅞" ribbon is good for experimenting, and ⅔ yard is long enough for any of the flowers.*

LOOPS *(figure 4.1). Fold the ribbon in half and tack. One loop is sufficient in some cases, but sometimes a double or triple loop is desired. When using ribbon wider than ½", gather across the base of the loop to pull it in.*

BOW *(figure 4.2). Overlap the ribbon as if to tie a bow and tack in the center. Several bows made of different-width ribbons can be stacked on top of each other to make a nosegay.*

STREAMERS *(figure 4.3). Allow the tails of bows to dangle a little longer than usual and tack in place to create loops (a). You will need to play with the ribbons, turning and twisting and pushing them into position (b). Use pins to hold the streamers until you can tack them to the background. Sometimes a ribbon will loop in one direction but not the other, so be patient. For tacking, use ordinary thread or try something decorative, like a French knot, a button, or a ribbon rose. When using ribbon ¾" or wider, gather the ribbon at each point where it is tacked down, as shown in "Fantasy Basket" pillow (photo 5).*

LOOPED CORDING *(figure 4.4). Cording will curve, twist, and turn easily; just arrange it and tack in place. It can be the backdrop for ribbon loops and buttons. It is applied to a seam on the button-adorned vest (photo 1).*

BEAD-RIBBON BORDER *(figure 4.5). Beads sewn down on top of ribbon make a great three-dimensional border. Set the beads about 1" apart and push up the ribbon in between them.*

RUCHING *(figure 4.6). In past times, dresses as well as hats were trimmed with ribbon ruching. Ruching will curve once it is made. To make ruching, hand-baste a zigzag pattern through the ribbon, then gently pull the thread (it will make a pointed effect as you pull). I have made ruching from ribbons ½" and wider.*

LAYERED LOOPS *(figure 4.7).*
*Make a long loop, then form a
second shorter loop on top (several
layers work fine); tack in place. Use
layered loops separately, or put two
together to create a bow.*

GATHERED FLOWERS
*(figure 4.8). These flowers are the
easiest of all the ribbon flowers to
make. They can be made with any
width ribbon, and several sizes can be
stacked on top of each other. To make
the basic flower (a), turn under the
raw edge of one end of the ribbon ¼"
and hand-gather along a long edge
until the ribbon forms a circle (b).
Pull in the gathers and knot the
thread twice. Trim the end if necessary, then lap the folded edge over the
raw edge and tack. Variations: (c)—
The ribbon gathers around itself,
forming a tight flower; (d)—French
wire-edged ribbon—pull the wire and
the ribbon gathers up into a circle;
(e)—A 1½" ribbon is folded in ⅜" on
one long edge and then gathered,
creating a raised effect in the center of
the ribbon. Another idea: Instead of
gathering the ribbon, pleat it, for a
flower that looks like a fan. You will
need to stitch through the pleats to
hold them.*

KNOTTED DAISY *(figure 4.9).*
*Use ⅜" ribbon. Tie a knot every 3",
dividing the ribbon into seven or
more sections. Fold each section in
half, overlapping the folds to make
the center of the flower. Tack with
needle and thread. The knots will end
up on the ends of the petals. Make at
least seven loops.*

ROSE *(figure 4.10). The ribbon rose
is best made with a double-faced satin
or taffeta ribbon. To form the center,
roll one end of the ribbon about six
turns to make a tube and tack with a
few stitches at the base (a). To form
the petals, fold the top edge of the
unwound ribbon down and toward
you at 45-degree angle (b). Using the
tacked base of the tube as a pivot, roll
the tube across the the fold, loosely at
the top and tightly at the bottom,
forming a cone shape (c). Tack the
base. Repeat the fold-turn-tack
process until the ribbon rose is as full
as you like (d).*

LEAVES *(figure 4.11). Fold a
narrow ribbon back on itself and tack
in place. If using wider ribbon as
shown here, gather the bottom edges to
give the leaf more dimension.*

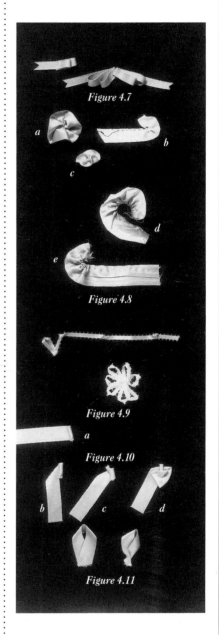

Figure 4.7

Figure 4.8

Figure 4.9

Figure 4.10

Figure 4.11

# Button and Trinket Imagery

**O**LD PEARL BUTTONS are my favorites, but in the last few years I have branched out and started using other types of buttons. The button-adorned vest (photo 1) is a good example of my daring! When you use buttons in clusters like I do, you need to be able to purchase them in bulk or find stashes of them in junk or antique stores. Martha Lewis, a quilting friend, has sent me many bags of old pearl buttons. My collection would get down to just a jar or two and along would come a package of buttons from Martha.

Old pearl buttons have a story to tell. Many still have the thread in the center from being cut off a garment. The back of these buttons is the imperfect side. Often it is rough in texture and shows the shell color. I like to sew these on so the back shows.

If the buttons are dirty, I put them in a jar with soap and water and soak them. Screw on the lid and shake the jar to help dislodge the dirt. Pearl buttons can be dyed with Rit dye. Purchase the liquid dye and start with one tablespoon of dye to two cups of hot water. Add the buttons. You may need to make the dye stronger. Wear rubber gloves while dyeing the buttons.

> I LIKE THE EFFECT OF BUTTONS PUSHED CLOSE TO EACH OTHER, OVERLAPPING, CREATING A THIRD DIMENSION.

## TRINKETS

A few trinkets sewn here and there or in a cluster of buttons work like a focal point by drawing attention to themselves. "Celebrate America" (photo 13) has stars, eagles, flags, and other tiny metal trinkets stitched to the top arcs. The charm vest (photo 32) is filled with hearts, keys, and cupids. Judith Montano, author of *The Crazy Quilt Handbook* and *Crazy Quilt Odyssey*, is the original user of charms in crazy quilting. Look to her books for inspiration.

## COMPOSITIONS

By combining buttons, trinkets, ribbons, and lace, you can achieve wonderful detailing. Below are five ideas that show you how. Most of the compositions on the quilts in chapter 7 involve several of these techniques and adornments.

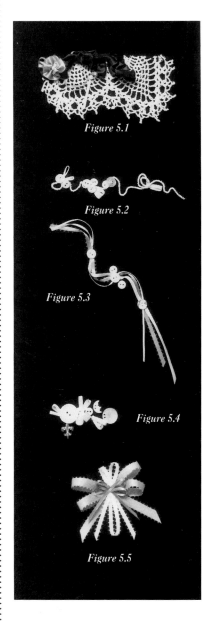

Figure 5.1

Figure 5.2

Figure 5.3

Figure 5.4

Figure 5.5

# *How to Layer It On*

1. *Always start with the larger item on the bottom and build from there. Place flat lace down first, then French silk ribbon, which can be crinkled to create a textured backdrop. Tack these in place. Sew ribbon vines and narrow ribbon loops on top of the French ribbon. A flower every so often finishes the look. Another finishing touch can be achieved with pearls (figure 5.1).*

2. *For a lovely freeform effect, try cording—it curves, twists, and turns easily. Tack down the cording first. Then add ribbon loops and top with layered buttons (figure 5.2).*

3. *Place two or three ribbons on a surface, winding and twisting them. As you tack them to the backing, sew on buttons. Or you might add tiny roses or pearls (figure 5.3).*

4. *Place ribbon loops down first. Then start layering the buttons, and add a charm here and there. This technique works best on projects with a cardboard or Thermolam fleece backing, such as in a pin or purse. The backing prevents the weight of the buttons from pulling the fabrics (figure 5.4).*

5. *Nosegays are layers of ribbon bows and loops, stacked on each other and stitched in the center. Top the very center with flowers, buttons, beads, or other favorite adornment (figure 5.5).*

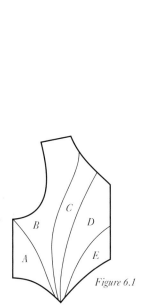

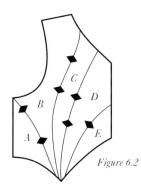

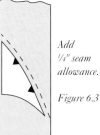

Add ¼" seam allowance.

*Figure 6.3*

Mark

*Figure 6.4*

*Figure 6.1*

*Figure 6.2*

# Stitched to Perfection

HE ART OF CURVED PIECING is not hard to master. As you look through the pictures of the projects, you will see some curved piecing. Being the practical person that I am, I experimented until I found a way that I could stitch pretty curves on the sewing machine without distortion. I first tried stitching to a foundation many years ago when I wanted tiny ¼" strips, and this technique has served as a base for many other projects.

Below are step-by-step instructions for foolproof curved piecing. I will use a vest as my example, but the technique can work for a quilt block, a pincushion, or any other project you might dream up.

## How to Sew Curved Piecing

1. *Trace the outside shape of the desired project (e.g., garment, quilt block) on tracing paper.*

2. *Sketch in the curved sections of the design, keeping inside the pattern outline. Make it a rule not to let the curves arc more than 45 degrees— they would be too difficult to machine- piece. A continuous curve tool can help you shape the curves and try out different designs.*

3. *Label each pattern section A, B, C, etc. (figure 6.1).*

4. *Mark notches every three inches on each seam line (figure 6.2).*

5. *Draw a small sketch of your design on a separate piece of paper for future reference. Be sure to label everything just as it is on the pattern.*

6. *Pin the paper pattern to muslin, flannel, or lightweight fleece and cut out along the outside shape. All of the piecing will be done on this fabric foundation. If your project will be lined, cut the lining now too.*

7. *Unpin the pattern from the founda- tion. Cut the paper pattern apart into its individual sections (on the curved lines you drew).*

8. *Place pattern A right side up on the right side of the chosen fabric, and pin. Cut out, adding ¼" seam allowance on the interior (notched) seam only (figure 6.3).*

9. *Using chalk or a marking pencil, mark all the matching notches by a dot within the ¼" seam allowance (figure 6.4).*

10. Continue cutting out and marking the remaining pieces in the same way. Leave the patterns pinned to the fabric. Arrange them in order on the work surface.

11. Place piece A in position on the foundation, referring to your small sketch as necessary. Carefully unpin and remove the pattern, then pin fabric A to the foundation.

12. Place piece B on fabric A, right sides facing and dots matching. Pin at dots through all layers. B will probably look like it isn't going to fit. Don't worry; it will.
NOTE: Before stitching, snip into concave (inside) curves about ⅛" every ¼" to fit nicely. Snipping consistently at equal intervals gives a more even curve.

13. Begin stitching the seam ¼" from the raw edges (figure 6.5). Take it slow, and remove pins before you get to them. I stitch an inch or two, then reposition the fabric. Gently ease the fabric as you stitch. A straight pin can be a helpful tool to push excess fabric to the side as you stitch. Concentrate on the seam you are stitching, and don't worry about the fabric to the left of the presser foot. Continue until the seam is finished.

14. Flip B over to the right side. It will seem to naturally take its place alongside A; stitching on a foundation keeps the seams in place. Continue adding the rest of the pattern pieces in the same way.

15. Unless I'm sewing a heavy, stubborn fabric, I wait until all the pieces are in place before pressing. Press in an up and down motion to cut down distortion.

## VARIATIONS

- Strip-piece fabric and place the pattern on top (figure 6.6). Try different angles to find the most interesting arrangement.
- Cover a section completely with a piece of lace. Or insert part of a doily on a section before adding the section next to it (figure 6.7).
- Insert premade piping between seams. First, stitch the piping to A (figure 6.8), then add B. To get in close, I use a zipper foot to stitch piping. Position the foot to the right of the needle and the piping to the left.
- Adorn seams with cording, ribbons, or trinkets (see the charm vest, photo 32).

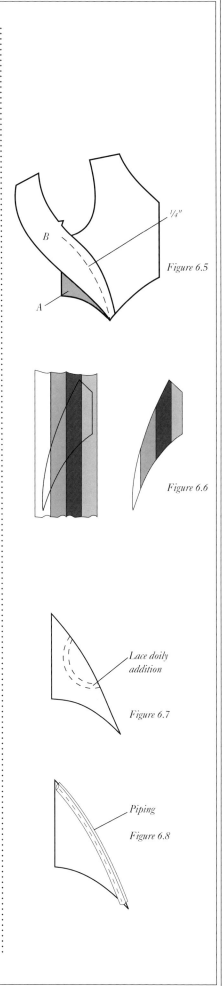

Figure 6.5

Figure 6.6

Lace doily addition

Figure 6.7

Piping

Figure 6.8

*Figure 6.9*

# DOODLE QUILTING

When I worked on the Victorian walking suit for the 1990 Fairfield Fashion Show, I let the quilting design develop from the curves of the laces I had appliquéd in place. I found my stitching just flowed along. This made for a very satisfying sewing experience, and the results were good. I have since used doodle quilting on the "Fantasy Basket" quilt (photo 7) and most of the layered appliqué projects (photos 6, 8, 9, and 10).

Doodle quilting seems to work well in spots where a repeated design does not exist. It reminds me of the flowing, curving lines you might see in a garden or ribbons in a heap on a table.

To work doodle quilting, choose a section of the appliqué where the shape bumps out and begin quilting along the edge (figure 6.9). Curve the quilting stitches around into a circle—you have created a new shape to quilt around when you pass through the area again. Echo quilting—repeating a line of stitching—helps create a sense of direction.

Doodle quilting lets you explore stitching and offers plenty of variety. On "Fantasy Basket" I quilted to keep with the flowing feeling of the ribbons, buttons, and laces. I started with the roses in the borders, sometimes following the stems, and let the lines go from there. I drew quilting lines on this quilt, but on the layered appliqué projects, I worked freehand from the start.

> DOODLE QUILTING JUST FLOWS— THE DESIGN DEVELOPS FROM THE CURVES AND POINTS OF THE PIECING AND LINENS.

# PIECED ARCS

Quilters have always admired New York Beauty quilts for the graphic quality of their intricately pieced arcs. But the construction can be intimidating at first sight. The basic block design, with an arc in one corner, is reminiscent of the fan block (figure 6.10). Piecing this arc accurately and keeping the points sharp is a challenge. Joanne Myers, a dear quilting friend of mine, developed a method of stitching the pieced arcs using a paper pattern. It has been student-tested in several classes with great success.

Joanne's flip-and-sew technique is like that used for strip piecing or paper-pieced pineapple blocks. The pattern is traced on lightweight paper, such as tracing paper or velum. Accuracy is ensured because all stitching is done on predrawn lines. Small stitches (20 to 25 per inch) prevent distortion when the paper is torn away.

# How to Piece an Arc

The patterns for this exercise are on pages 75–77. (To order preprinted arc patterns, see Sources, page 95.) Use patterns B, C, and D for a large arc or BB, CC, and DD for a small arc.

1. Trace the entire pieced arc B [BB] onto lightweight paper. Cut out on the cutting line.
2. From contrasting fabrics, cut two strips 44" by 1¾". Place the strips together, right sides facing, with the lighter value fabric on top.
3. Place arc pattern B [BB] on top of the fabric strips, right side up, so that the raw fabric edges extend ¼" to the right of the leftmost point and the top of the strips extends ½" above the paper pattern (figure 6.11).
4. Set your sewing machine for 20 to 25 stitches to the inch. Beginning at the top edge of the paper, stitch on the marked line through all layers until the bottom of the paper is reached. Be sure to stitch exactly on the pattern line for a point that is sharp and perfect.
5. Flip the dark fabric to the right, over the seam allowances, and press lightly with a dry iron. Trim the excess fabric top and bottom even with the pattern cutting line. Trim the seam allowances evenly to ¼".
6. With the pattern facing you, place the light strip underneath the dark piece, right sides facing. Line up the raw edge of the light strip so it extends ¼" beyond the seam line drawn on the pattern. Make sure

the strip extends ½" above the paper pattern. Pin in place (figure 6.12).
7. Stitch through the paper and the fabric as before. Flip the light fabric to the right. Trim the excess dark fabric ¼" from the seam line and at the top and bottom. You've just completed one point.
8. Continue alternating light and dark fabrics, trimming after each seam, until the arc is completed.
9. Press well. Do not remove the paper at this time.
10. To cut A [AA], place pattern D [DD] on an 11¼" [4½"] square of fabric, matching corners and sides. Mark and cut curve (figure 6.13). Discard corner piece. Cut out C [CC] from pattern.
11. To add A [AA] to the pieced arc, mark the center of each curved edge with a pin. Place A and B [AA and BB] together, right sides facing, with pins matching. Line up the straight edges and pin at each end. This assemblage will look awkward. You may need to clip the inside curve (figure 6.14) and add more pins. Stitch, paper side up, on the seam line indicated.
12. Repeat step 11 to add C [CC].
13. Carefully remove the paper; a straight pin helps to "grab" it. Press the completed block.

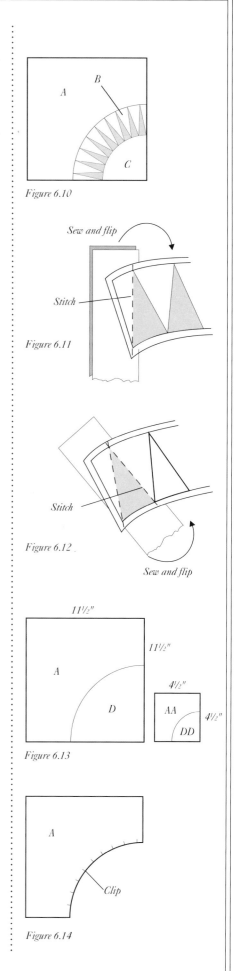

Figure 6.10

Sew and flip

Stitch

Figure 6.11

Stitch

Figure 6.12

Sew and flip

11½"    11½"

A

D    4½"

AA    4½"

DD

Figure 6.13

A

Clip

Figure 6.14

CHAPTER SEVEN

# Projects and Patterns

*Yardages are for 44" fabrics. Patterns are on pages 75–93. All patterns include a ¼" seam allowance unless otherwise indicated. For project photos, see pages 49–64.*

## QUILTS

### EVENING SKY

*Joanne Myers made this New York Beauty quilt using a method of paper piercing that she devised (see page 25). The finished arcs are absolutely perfect. When I saw Joanne making this quilt, I pictured it with the added softness of Battenberg lace. Joanne consented to let me purchase it, we added the lace, and she finished it. The lace embellishment set Joanne's creative mind to work; she repeated a design in the lace for the quilting motif, then accented it with echo quilting. The quilt captures the mood and colors of central Oregon skies at sunset—one of my favorite scenes. Photo 37; finished size, 58" x 60¾".*

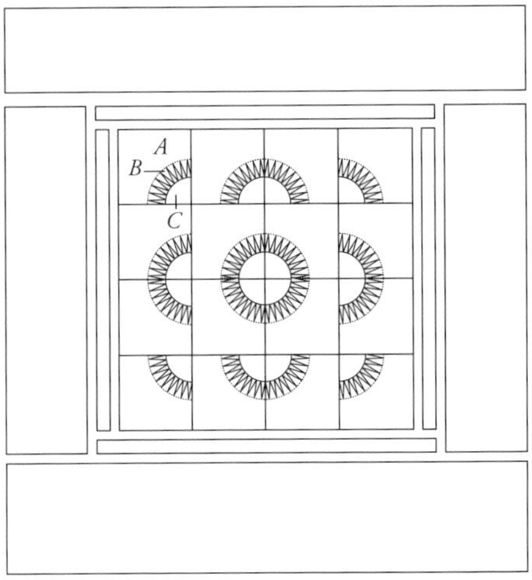


*Figure 7.1—Evening Sky*

#### MATERIALS (see figure 7.1):

This quilt is scrappy in nature. The yardage listed below for fabrics A, B, and C refers to the total needed for each section. For a more interesting quilt, use a variety of fabrics to make up the total. Joanne Myers cut her 16 A sections from eleven different fabrics.

| | |
|---|---|
| A | 2 yards |
| B | ⅞ yard light, ⅞ yard dark |
| C | ⅓ yard |
| piping fabric | ¼ yard |
| ⅛" cording | 5¼ yard |
| 1st border fabric | ¼ yard |
| 2nd border fabric | 1⅓ yards |
| backing fabric | 3½ yards |
| batting | 61" x 64" |
| binding fabric | ⅓ yard |
| 2½" flat lace | (optional) 1⅔ yards |
| 10" circle doilies | (optional) 2 |
| template plastic | |

#### CUTTING GUIDE:

Patterns are on pages 75–76.

| | |
|---|---|
| A | 16 (use 11¼" squares) |
| B | 16 light and 16 dark strips, 1¾" x 44" |
| C | 16 |
| piping | 4 strips 1½" x 44" |
| 1st border | 5 strips 1½" x 44" |
| 2nd border sides, top | 4 strips 6¼" x 44" |
| 2nd border bottom | 2 strips 9" x 44" |
| backing | 44" x 61" and 13½" x 61" |
| binding | 6 strips 1¾" x 44" |

#### Assembly:

1. Sew 16 New York Beauty blocks following the instructions on page 25. Blocks should measure 11¼" x 11¼".

2. Optional: Attach doily and lace insets to A and C segments. Round doilies can be cut into quarters, placed on C, and stitched into the seams. Lace yardage can be placed on A after A and B have been stitched together. The laces should be tacked in place with matching thread about every ¾".

3. Arrange blocks on a flat surface (see figure 7.1). Stitch together in rows of four blocks each. Press seams. Stitch four rows together to form quilt center.

4. Stitch the four piping strips end to end to make one long strip. Fold strip over the ⅛" cording and stitch close to cording with a zipper foot. Beginning at the enter of one quilt side and using zipper foot, sew piping to the quilt edge all around. Turn the piping at the corners as close to a 45-degree angle as you can. Overlap the piping as you finish sewing, and trim off the loose ends.

5. Stitch the five 1st border strips end to end to make one long strip. From this piece, cut two 43½" strips and add to quilt sides. Cut two 46" strips and add to quilt top and bottom.

6. Stitch the first four 2nd border strips to make one long strip. Cut two 46" strips and add to quilt sides. Cut one 58" strip and add to quilt top.

7. Stitch the two remaining 2nd border strips together for one long strip. Cut one 58" strip and add to quilt bottom.

8. Mark the quilting design on the top and layer the quilt. Quilt by hand or machine.

9. Stitch the six binding strips together for one long strip and bind quilt edges.

# ROSY YELLOW

*Barbara Slater made the four center blocks of this New York Beauty variation in one of Joanne's classes. I was so taken with the colors that I asked her if I could create a border and feature it in the book. The smaller border arcs fit perfectly in scale. Joanne Myers did the border arrangement and machine quilting. This small quilt turned into a real group effort. Photo 34; finished size, 32½" x 32½".*

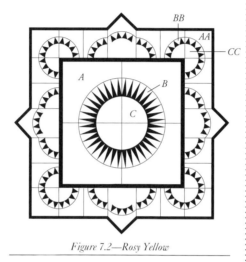

*Figure 7.2—Rosy Yellow*

MATERIALS (see figure 7.2):

| | |
|---|---|
| A, C, AA, CC | 1 yard |
| B, BB | ¾ yard light |
| B, BB, inside border, binding fabric | 1 yard dark |
| backing fabric | 1 yard |
| batting | 34" x 34" |
| template plastic | |

## CUTTING GUIDE:

Patterns are on pages 75–77.

| | |
|---|---|
| A | 4 (use 9¼" squares) |
| B | 4 light and 4 dark strips, 1¼" x 44" |
| C | 4 |
| inside border | 3 strips 1¼" x 44" |
| AA | 24 (use 4½" squares) |
| BB | 8 light and 8 dark strips, 2" x 44 |
| CC | 24 |
| border inserts | four 4½" x 3" |
| backing | 35" x 35" |
| binding | 3 strips 1¼" x 44" |

❦ Assembly:

1. Sew 4 large (A-B-C) and 24 small (AA-BB-CC) New York Beauty blocks following the instructions on page 25. Blocks should measure 9¼" x 9¼" and 4½" x 4½". You can add doily and lace insets (see "Evening Sky," step 2) if you wish.

2. Join the 4 large blocks together as shown in figure 7.2.

3. Stitch the inside border strips end to end to make one long strip. From this piece, cut two 18" strips and add to quilt sides. Cut two 20½" strips and add to quilt top and bottom.

4. Make the four angled blocks: Pin a pieced block on point on a border insert (figure 7.3). Appliqué, turning under the edges ¼". Trim excess fabric behind the appliqué.

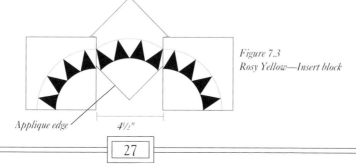

Figure 7.3
Rosy Yellow—Insert block

Applique edge    4½"

5. Arrange the border blocks (figure 7.2). Stitch five blocks together for top and bottom borders and add to quilt. Stitch remaining blocks together for the side borders and add to quilt.

6. Mark the top for quilting. Layer the quilt and quilt by hand or machine. Joanne followed the floral pattern in the fabric and outline-quilted the arcs.

7. Stitch the three binding strips together for one long strip and bind quilt edges; you will need to tuck and hand-stitch where the points meet the quilt edge.

## HEART BUTTON COLLECTION

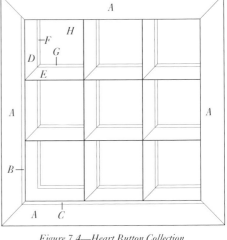

*Figure 7.4—Heart Button Collection*

*I suppose it is only natural that I would collect heart-shaped buttons, since hearts are my most favorite motif and sewing is both my work and my pleasure.*

*The buttons resurfaced in my sewing room several times before I figured out a way to use them on a quilt surface. My dilemma was finding a pieced design that would truly highlight the collection. One day I happened onto the heart-shaped crocheted doilies, and the attic window design clicked.*

*Attic window is a great way to feature a special fabric or a collection as it provides neat compartments on the quilt surface. The heart doilies found a place in the windowpanes, and the buttons naturally fell onto the window sash—in fact, their scale helped me determine the sash width. Sorting the buttons into like categories helped the quilt design along. There were enough large buttons to serve as "cornerstones." I realized that the weight of so many buttons would make the fabric sag, so I decided early in the project to have the finished quilt professionally framed.*

*To set off the buttons, I used linen for the blocks and outer borders and moiré for the muntins. These nontraditional fabrics created a subtle, textured backdrop. I added ⅛" pink silk ribbons to further accent the pink in the quilt. Silk ribbons are very pliable and make possible the twists and turns I wanted to achieve to help the design flow. Photo 31; finished size, 25" x 25" (including frame).*

❦ Assembly:

1. To construct the attic window block, you will be using the Y seam construction. Make plastic templates for DF and EG using patterns on page 92.

2. Stitch D to F along the 44" length. Repeat with E and G. Press toward the wider strip.

3. Lay template DF on strip DF, making sure that fabric F and the shorter edge of the template are aligned (figure 7.5). Cut 9. Repeat with template EG and strip EG, with fabric G on the shorter edge (figure 7.6).

4. Place DF on the left side of H, right sides facing. Stitch a ¼" seam from the top of the block to within ¼" of the raw edge (figure 7.7a). Stop!

MATERIALS (see figure 7.4):

| | |
|---|---|
| A, H | ⅝ yard |
| B, F | ⅛ yard |
| C, G | ⅛ yard |
| D, E | ¼ yard |
| Thermolam fleece | 26" x 26" |
| template plastic | |
| ⅛" silk ribbon | 2 yards light, |
| | 1¼ yards dark, |
| | 1 yard contrasting |
| ¼" silk | |
| ribbon garland | (optional) |
| 3" heart-shaped | |
| doilies | 9 |
| buttons ⅜" or | |
| smaller, for | |
| corner nosegay | 32 |
| button collection | approximately 120 |
| | pieces |
| frame | (optional) |

CUTTING GUIDE:

| | |
|---|---|
| A | 4 strips 4½" x 25¼" (includes framing allowance) |
| B, C | 1 strip ¼" x 25¼" |
| D, E | 4 strips 1¼" x 44" |
| F, G | 4 strips ¾" x 44" |
| H | 9 blocks 4½" x 4½" |

5. Place EG on the bottom of H, right sides facing. Stitch from the lower right corner to the same spot where you stopped stitching before (figure 7.7b).

6. Place DF and EG together, right sides facing. Insert the needle at the spot where you stopped stitching and stitch to the outside edge. You have just completed the Y seam construction (figure 7.7c). Finished block size is 5½" x 5½". Repeat steps 4–6 to make nine attic window blocks.

7. Join the blocks in three rows of three blocks each (see figure 7.4 for placement). Then join the three rows.

8. Stitch B to an A along long edge. Repeat to join C to an A. (Two A's stay plain.) Press toward the wider strip.

9. Use the 45-degree angle on your ruler to miter-cut the corners of borders A, AB, and AC (figure 7.8). Sew these pieces to the quilt using the Y seam construction.

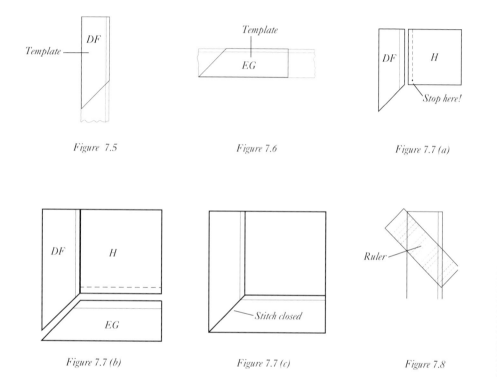

Figure 7.5

Figure 7.6

Figure 7.7 (a)

Figure 7.7 (b)

Figure 7.7 (c)

Figure 7.8

10. Center the quilt top on the Thermolam fleece. Stitch in the ditch through the main seams in the blocks to stabilize the top.

11. Place the doilies in the blocks and tack down.

12. Arrange the buttons and stitch them in place.

13. Stitch the ribbons in place (see chapter 4 for techniques) and add buttons to the nosegay.

## MATERIALS (see figure 7.9):

The quilt top is lightweight linen, and the hearts are novelty taffeta, polished cotton, satin, and hankies.

| | |
|---|---|
| A (background fabric for quilt top) | 1 yard |
| B, piping fabric | ½ yard |
| C, E | ⅛ yard each of three different fabrics, can include hankies |
| D | 1 hanky with symmetrical designs in all four corners, or 3 hankies, each with a corner design |
| backing fabric | 1 yard |
| Thermolam fleece | 25" x 36" |
| ⅛" preshrunk cording | 3¼ yards |
| narrow decorative cording for top row of buttons | 2 yards |
| buttons ⅝"or smaller, for top row and along vine | 80 to 100 |
| 3" crocheted lace | ⅔ yard |
| ¼" ribbon for bows on lace | 2 yards |
| ¼" buttons for bows | 8 |

metallic gold quilting thread

wax-coated freezer paper for appliqué

NOTE: Try a variety of ribbons for loops and bows—here are the sizes and quantities I used:

| | |
|---|---|
| assorted ⅛" ribbons for loops | 3 yards total |
| ¼" ribbon for loops and vine | 2 yards |
| picot-edged, textured, and plain satin ribbons, ⅜" wide | 2½ yards total |

## CUTTING GUIDE:

Patterns are on pages 78–79. To make quilt top A and backing, cut a 23½" x 33½" rectangle from the appropriate fabric. Fold in half vertically to measure 11¾" x 33½". Place the top "dip" pattern along fold and touching top fabric edge—mark and cut to achieve the top shape. Place the bottom "bump" pattern along fold at bottom edge—mark and cut horizontally all the way to the side edges. Using a teacup or other circle-shaped object, mark curves on the four corners and trim. To prepare the hearts for needleturn appliqué, cut hearts without seam allowance from freezer paper as follows: B: 1, C: 4, D: 3, E: 10. With a dry iron, iron freezer paper shiny side down to the wrong side of the fabric or hankies chosen for the hearts and cut out ¼" beyond the edge of the paper.

| | |
|---|---|
| piping | 1½" x 117" bias strip (piece as necessary) |

# A PORTRAIT OF HEARTS

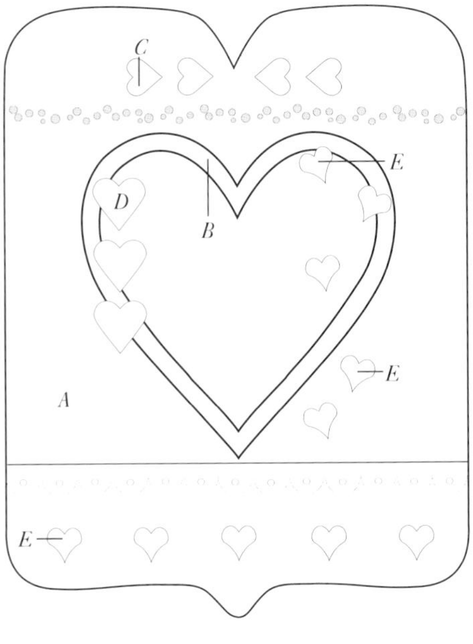

*Figure 7.9—A Portrait of Hearts*

*This "heart portrait" is truly an intimate quilt. It must be viewed up close and is best displayed in a small, cozy setting or above a piece of furniture. Many different fabrics, ribbons, and buttons create textural interest on the quilt surface, and hand quilting in gold thread adds the ultimate touch.*

*Hearts are everywhere in this quilt. From the very beginning, I had in mind to somehow echo the heart shape in the quilt edge—I was able to bring out this subtle accent with piping. Several hankies from my grandmother made their way into the design, though they are hardly recognizable in their new heart shapes. Patterns for the three hearts on the left side of the quilt were positioned to capture a hanky's corner repeats. Some of the hearts at the top and right feature overall designs from other hankies. Study the designs on your hankies carefully so that you can choose shapes and pattern placements that will show them off.*

*A friend of mine, Patty Bentley, helped me when I was terribly stuck on the quilt design. I had placed the hearts in the center portion of the quilt and was searching for a border to divide them into two groups. It just wasn't working. Patty took one look at the quilt and suggested the large heart shape that encompasses the entire center section. It was just what the design needed. From there, the quilt was on its way. Photo 36; finished size, 23" x 33" (measured from top to tip).*

### Assembly:

1. Study photo 36 for the position of hearts and trims.
2. Place the hearts in position on the background fabric. Hand-appliqué heart B first, then hearts C, D, and E. Carry the thread on the wrong side, coming up just enough to catch the heart. Use your needle to turn the raw edges under at the inside curve. After going around a heart, slit the background fabric behind the heart just enough to pull out the freezer paper. For more information, see the excellent reference, *Appliqué 12 Easy Ways!* by Elly Sienkiewicz.
3. Place the quilt top on the Thermolam fleece, and baste around the edges.
4. Add the crocheted lace and tack in place.
5. Create the corded and looped border following the instructions on page 18. Sew on the buttons in clusters.
6. Form eight bows from 7½" lengths of ribbon. Tack the bows to the crocheted lace, topping each bow with a button.
7. Using ¼" and ⅜" ribbons to form loops and vines, connect the five E hearts on the right side of the quilt in a graceful, twining effect; follow the instructions on page 18. Buttons are sewn on as if scattered to accentuate the flow of the vine.

8. To make piping, fold the bias strip over the ⅛" cording and stitch close to the cording with a zipper foot.

9. Place the piping on the right side of the quilt ¼" from the edge. Start at the top center and leave ½" of piping extending (figure 7.10). Using the zipper foot, stitch all around, letting piping overlap at the center. Clip at the corners and curves.

*Figure 7.10*

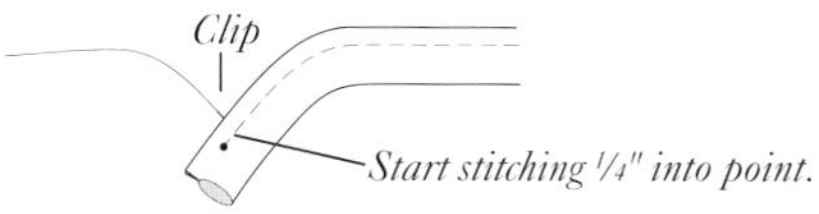


10. Place the the quilt top and backing together, right sides facing. Still using the zipper foot, stitch around the edge over the seam just stitched. Leave a 6" opening at the top for turning. Trim off excess fabric, and turn the quilt to the right side. Hand-stitch the opening closed.

11. Look at photo 36 for quilting ideas. The center heart is worked in a 1" grid set on the diagonal. Two rows of outline quilting surround each heart. You can work quilting by hand or machine.

## FANTASY BASKET

*This fan-shaped basket block is a variation of the traditional Grandmother's Fan. The outside fan blades are rounded asymmetrically, a heart adorns the base, and a stand and handle complete the transition from fan to basket. I used as many different ribbon techniques as I could think of to decorate these sampler baskets! Fabrics were kept simple to allow the ribbon embellishment to stand out as a focal point.*

*Sashing in two colors acts almost like a trellis in a flower garden. Mary Jahns worked the curvy, rambling hand quilting to echo the free floral feeling of the fabric. Photo 7; finished size, 35" x 58".*

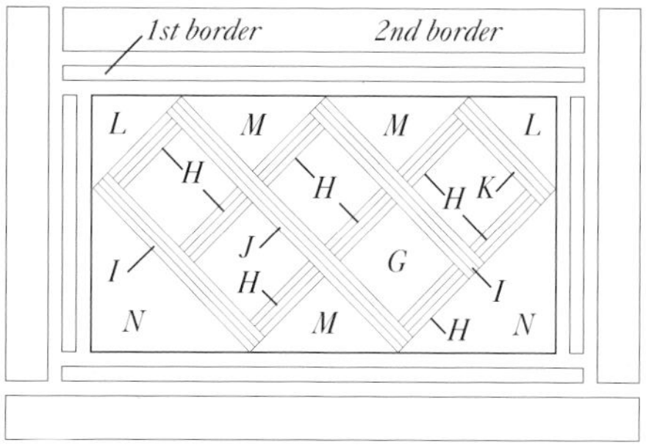


*Figure 7.11—Fantasy Basket*

### Assembly:

Basket block (make 5):

1. Following figure 7.12, sew 2 of A, 2 of B, and 1 of C together, ending with a tack stitch ¼" from the top (curved) edge. Press seams open.

2. Lay block G on point on a flat surface, and center the fan and handle F on it; test-fit the stand pieces E and make sure you allow enough room for them. You may need to trim the ends of the handle to fit when the edges of the fan are turned under.

3. Appliqué the handle, sides, and top of the fan. Turn the edges under as you stitch or use freezer paper as described in "A Portrait of Hearts" (cutting guide and step 2).

4. Stitch a stand E to each side of heart D (figure 7.13), ending ¼" from the top of the stand.

5. Position the heart-stand piece on the base of the fan, remembering that the edges will be turned under ¼". Insert lace under the heart if desired, then appliqué the heart-stand.

### MATERIALS (see figure 7.11):

| | |
|---|---|
| A, B, C, 2nd border, backing fabric | 2½ yards |
| D | ⅛ yard each of two different fabrics |
| E, F | ¼ yard |
| G, L, M, N, light sashing fabric | 1¾ yards |
| dark sashing, 1st border, binding fabric | ¾ yard |
| batting | 37" x 60" |

NOTE: An assortment of ribbons, lace, and buttons adorns this sampler. Listed below are the sizes and quantities I used:

| | |
|---|---|
| grosgrain, satin, feather-edge, and picot-edge ribbons, up to ¾" wide | 5 yards total |
| flat lace, up to ½" wide | 3 yards |
| pieces of doilies (to tuck under hearts) | |
| buttons, ⅞" or smaller | 50 to 60 |
| narrow cording | 2 yards each of two colors |

### CUTTING GUIDE:

Patterns are on page 80.

| | |
|---|---|
| A | 10 (reverse 5) |
| B | 10 |
| C | 5 |
| D | 5, from the two fabrics |
| E | 10 |
| F | 5 |
| G | 5 blocks 10½" x 10½" |
| light sashing | 5 strips 1" x 44" |
| dark sashing | 10 strips 1" x 44" |
| L | 1 block 10" x 10", cut in half diagonally |
| M | 2 blocks 12" x 12", cut in half diagonally |
| N | 1 block 18" x 18", cut in half diagonally |
| 1st border | 4 strips 1" x 44" |
| 2nd border | 5 strips 4" x 44" |
| backing | 35" x 58" |
| binding | 5 strips 1¾" x 44" |

6. Embellish the baskets with as many different lace, button, ribbon techniques as you choose to create your own sampler. Refer to chapters 3, 4, and 5 and photo 7 for ideas.

Joining and finishing:

7. To make sashing, sew one light and two dark strips together (figure 7.14). From these five pieced strips, cut 8 H 10½" long, 2 I 25" long, 1 J 36½" long, and 1 K 13" long.

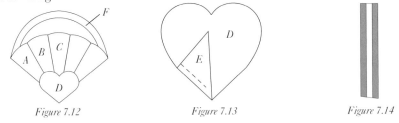

*Figure 7.12*          *Figure 7.13*          *Figure 7.14*

8. Lay the blocks, sashing, and background pieces L, M, and N on a large flat surface, following figure 7.11. Stitch together in diagonal rows, adding the N's last.

9. Stitch four 1st border strips end to end to make one long strip. From this piece, cut two 26½" strips and add to quilt sides. Cut two 50½" strips and stitch to quilt top and bottom.

10. Stitch five 2nd border strips to make one long strip. Cut two 27¾" strips and add to quilt sides. Cut two 58½" strips and add to quilt top and bottom.

11. Layer the quilt and work the quilting. Hand doodle quilting was used here.

12. Stitch five binding strips to make one long strip. Bind the quilt, allowing ½" of binding to show on the quilt top (to match the width of the 1st border).

## MATERIALS (see figure 7.15):

| | |
|---|---|
| fabric for border, plain block, binding, backing | 2 yards |
| 5 black prints | ¼ yard each |
| 2 light-background fabrics | ¼ yard each |
| 3" crocheted hearts | 3 |
| 8" hanky with all-around border | 1 |
| ¾" flat lace | ⅔ yard |
| 4" flat lace | ½ yard |
| ⅝" picot-edged ribbon | ¾ yard |
| 6" lace doily | 1 |
| buttons, ¼" or smaller | 80 to 100 |
| special embellishment for plain block | (optional) |
| batting | 33" x 33" |

## CUTTING GUIDE:

Patterns are on pages 81–83. The blocks have a scrappy look and are pieced from random fabrics, except for the crazypatch blocks, which are pieced to match. To cut fabrics for piecing, refer to photo 29 and figures 7.15–7.22, and choose your own fabrics.

**Star block**

| | | |
|---|---|---|
| A | 3 squares 3½" x 3½" | |
| B | 12 rectangles 2" x 3½" | |
| C | 24 squares 2" x 2" | |
| D | 12 squares 2" x 2" | |

**Heart block**

| | | |
|---|---|---|
| E, H | 4 | |
| F, G | 8 (reverse 4) | |

**Crazypatch block**

| | | |
|---|---|---|
| I, J, K, L, M, N | 4 | |
| foundation | 4 squares 6½" x 6½" (use scrap fabric) | |

**Fan block**

| | | |
|---|---|---|
| O, Q, R | 4 | |
| P | 8 (reverse 4) | |
| border | 2 strips 4½" x 24½", 2 strips 4½" x 32½" | |
| backing | 33" x 33" | |
| binding | 4 strips 1¼" x 35" | |

## FOUR-BLOCK SAMPLER

*Six-inch blocks are a great size to work with in smaller quilts. For this sampler quilt, I designed fan, heart, and crazypatch blocks, then added a traditional sawtooth star block as a fourth.*

*All of the crazypatch blocks are alike. I drafted one pattern and stitched the pieces in succession by chaining the blocks together, just like I do for geometric*

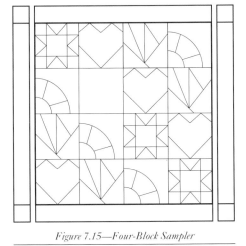

*Figure 7.15—Four-Block Sampler*

*repeats. You only have to make decisions once when the blocks are alike.*

*And talk about odd collections—Carrol Clark had given me an unusual thimble holder-pincushion crocheted on a wishbone! Wanting to display it was the starting point of this sampler quilt, and I left one block plain for just this purpose. I have quite a collection of black and cream fabric, and the laces and pearl buttons worked well with these, the pincushion, and each other. The beautiful hanky divided among the four corners was a gift from another quilter. Ursula Searles did the machine quilting. Photo 29; finished size, 31" x 31".*

## ❦ Assembly:

Star block (make 3):

1. Fold C in half diagonally, press the fold, and open. Place C on B, right sides facing, matching edges, and stitch on the fold. Trim ¼" beyond the seam allowance (figure 7.16a).

2. Place a second C on the free end of B-C. Stitch on the fold and trim as before. Repeat steps 1 and 2 assembly line–style for 12 C-B-C patches (figure 7.16b).

3. Following figure 7.17, join A, C-B-C, and D patches in rows, then join rows together for 3 star blocks.

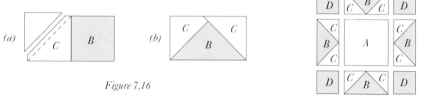

*Figure 7.16*

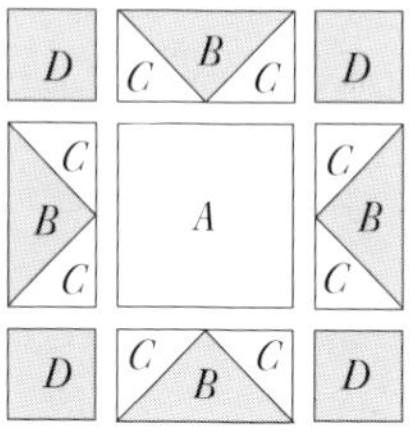

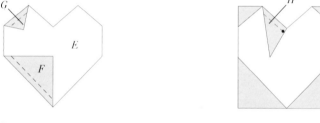

*Figure 7.17—Star Block*

Heart block (make 4)

4. Place F and G on E, right sides facing, and stitch (figure 7.18). Repeat on opposite side. Press seams open.

5. Place H on E, right sides facing, dots matching at top center of heart (figure 7.19). Stitch to the dot on one side. Remove from the sewing machine, and clip almost to the dot. Line up the other side of the heart and stitch from the dot to the outer edge. Repeat to make four heart blocks.

*Figure 7.18—Heart Block*

*Figure 7.19*

Crazypatch block (make 4)

6. Lay the four foundation squares on a flat surface. Referring to figure 7.20, place I pieces in position on each square and pin. Place J on I, right sides facing and edges matching. Stitch ¼" from raw edge. Flip J to the right side (figure 7.21).

*Figure 7.20—Crazypatch Block*

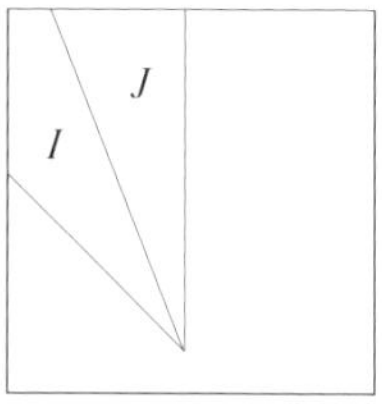

*Figure 7.21*

7. Chain the four blocks together one after the other for more streamlined construction.

8. Repeat step 6 to add pieces K, L, M, and N. Add any trims as you finish each section so that the raw edges are covered by the next seam. Press.

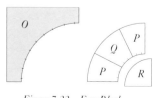

*Figure 7.22—Fan Block*

MATERIALS (see figure 7.23):

| | |
|---|---|
| pieced cow head | 1/8 yard |
| pieced cow body | 1/4 yard |
| A, AA, AAA, K, L, M, V, X, binding | 2/3 yard |
| cow fabric for B, optional prairie point lining | 1/4 yard |
| C, Q, R | 1/8 yard |
| E, SS, 1, 2, 3, 4, 5, 6, 7, 8 | 1/4 yard |
| F, J, N, P, S | 1/4 yard |
| D, G, I, O, T, W | 1/8 yard |
| H | preprinted cow panel 6" x 7" |
| U cow fabric | 1/3 yard |
| Y, Z (border) | 3/8 yard |
| backing fabric | 3/4 yard |
| fusible webbing (optional for prairie point lining) | 1/3 yard |
| batting | 30" x 32" |

six-strand embroidery floss for tail of cow
collection of cow memorabilia; greeting card is approximately 4" x 6"

CUTTING GUIDE:

As each piece is cut, label with Post-It note or masking tape.

**Pieced cow block**

| | |
|---|---|
| body | 4" x 6" |
| legs | two 2" x 2" |
| head | 2" x 3" |
| ears, 1 | 1 7/8" x 1 7/8", cut in half diagonally (figure 7.24) |
| 2, 3 | 2" x 3" |
| 4 | 1 1/2" x 4 1/2" |
| 5, 6 | 1 1/2" x 5 1/2" |
| 7 | 1" x 10 1/2" |
| 8 | 1 1/2" x 10 1/2". |
| A, C | 1 1/2" x 6" |
| AA | 2 strips 1" x 23 1/2" |
| B | 6" x 11" |
| D, G, I | 1" x 6" |
| E, F | 3 1/4" x 3 1/4" |
| H | 6" x 7" |
| J | eleven 5" x 5" |
| prairie point lining | 6 squares 5" x 5", cut in half diagonally |
| K | 3" x 21" |
| L, M | 1" x 12 1/2" |
| N | 1" x 7 1/2" |
| O, P | 4" x 4" |
| Q | two 1 1/2" x 7 1/2" |
| R | two 1 1/2" x 3 1/2" |
| S | 1 1/2" x 4 1/2" |
| SS | 3 1/2" x 1 1/2" |
| T | 1" x 7 1/2" |
| U | 6 1/2" x 11" |
| V | 3" x 15" |
| W | 2 1/2" x 7" |
| X | 2" x 13 1/2" |
| Y | two 3" x 27" |
| Z | two 3" x 29" |
| binding | 3 strips 1 1/4" x 44" |
| backing | 30" x 32" |

Fan block (make 4)

9. Stitch 2 P's to each Q, right sides facing, along straight edges. Press.

10. Using the arc joining technique (page 25, steps 11–12), sew O and R to P-Q-P. Clip in 1/8" every 1/4" along the curved edge of O and the bottom curved edge of P-Q-P (figure 7.22). Clipping evenly ensures a smooth finished seam. Mark the center of each curve with a pin. Match up the pins and pin through all layers. Match the straight side edges and pin.

11. With the clipped piece facing up, carefully stitch a 1/4" seam. Don't worry about the excess fabric to the left of the needle. Stitch an inch or so, then stop and reposition the fabric if necessary. Repeat to make four blocks.

Joining and finishing:

12. Add laces and ribbons to the individual blocks.

13. Referring to figure 7.15, arrange the blocks on a flat surface. Join together in rows, then join the rows to each other.

14. Sew the two shorter border strips at top and bottom, then sew the two longer side borders. Pin a hanky in each corner and stitch in place.

15. Place the quilt top on the batting and pin. Stitch on buttons through both layers; see chapter 5.

16. Layer the quilt. Quilt by hand or machine. Stitch the four binding strips together for one long strip and bind quilt edges.

## COWS, COWS, AND MOO COWS

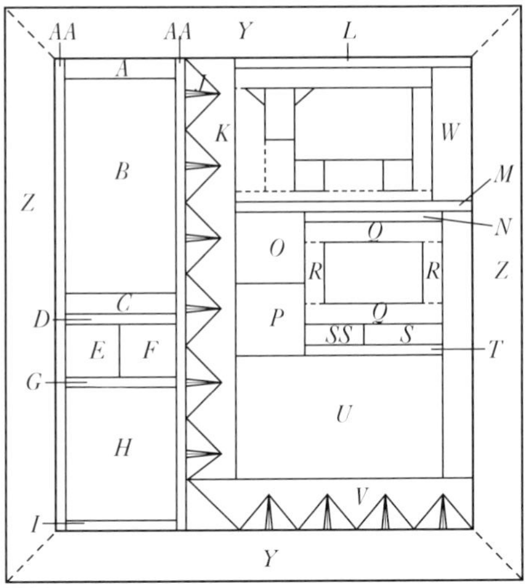

*Figure 7.23—Cows, Cows, and Moo Cows*

*June Jaeger writes: Cows have always had a soft spot in my heart. The walls and shelves of my kitchen are covered with cows—not just black and white milk cows but other cows as well! In time, I realized that my growing cow collection included pins, earrings, buttons, and fabric. I wanted a special place to display everything, and that is how this cow quilt came about.*

*My cows are everywhere! I stitched a cow greeting card directly to the fabric, pieced a cow block, and used cow fabric in the prairie point trim. The floral border helps frame all the cow memorabilia—as if my cows are grazing in a field of flowers.*

*I found as I worked that I needed 1/2" "stretcher strips" to prevent one area from running into another. These simple fabric strips can also be used to help blocks line up with each other. I start by sewing an unchangeable area, such as the pieced cow, a postcard, or a cross-stitch picture, and work out one section at a time. Sometimes, I simply leave the edge of a block unstitched until another section is joined. A computerized sewing machine with the alphabet let me write on blocks. And when I couldn't find the right stencil, I used rubber stamps with great results. Photo 11; finished size, 27" x 29".*

## ❧ Assembly:

1. Piece the cow block: Sew one ear to piece 1 along diagonal edge. Press toward the ear fabric. Place this pieced section right side up in the top left corner of the cow body. Flip back the ear to expose the seams, then use the seam edge as a guide to draw a diagonal cutting line across the corner of the cow body. Trim on this line (figure 7.25). Place remaining cow ear on body, right sides facing and diagonal edges matching, and stitch; press toward ear. Follow the piecing diagram (figure 7.26) to assemble the cow block. Join legs to 2, head to 3, and ear-1 to 4. Join these four sections, sewing body to leg section first. Add borders 5, 6, 7, and 8. For tail, cut embroidery floss to the length desired and hand-stitch in place.

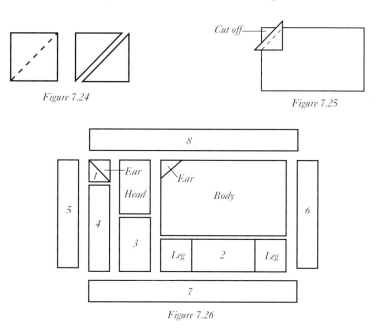

Figure 7.24

Figure 7.25

Figure 7.26

2. Make prairie points (figure 7.27): Fold J in half diagonally (a), then fold two outside points to the center (b). Press. Pin prairie points along the long edges of K and V; points may overlap a little bit. Trim off excess fabric (c). Fold remaining J in half diagonally and pin on lower left corner of V (see figure 7.23). The prairie points and corner piece will be joined in when the seams are sewn.

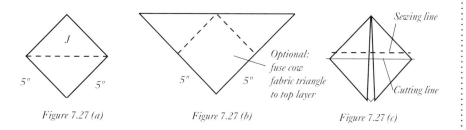

Figure 7.27 (a)

Figure 7.27 (b)

Figure 7.27 (c)

3. Stitch R and Q borders to postcard. Use a long hand-basting stitch to prevent card from tearing.

4. Assemble the quilt section by section (postcard section, left cow panel, etc.) and then join sections with strips (refer to figure 7.23 for placement).

5. Mitre-cut a 45-degree angle on borders Y and Z and add to the quilt using the Y seam construction (see pages 28–29, steps 1–6).

6. Layer the quilt. Quilt by hand or machine, and add buttons and pins. Stitch the three binding strips end to end to make one long strip and bind quilt edges.

MATERIALS (see figure 7.28):

| | |
|---|---|
| light backgrounds for A, I, L, S, W | ⅓ yard each three different fabrics |
| dark backgrounds for C, M, Y | ⅓ yard each two different fabrics |
| medium backgrounds for E, G, J, O, U | ⅓ yard each two different fabrics |
| narrow borders B, D, F, H, K, N, P, R, T, V, X, Z, AA, BB, CC, DD | ¼ yard |
| EE | ⅛ yard |
| 1¼" trim for Q, FF | 2⅜ yards |
| ⅛" ribbon for frame in block S | 1 yard |
| assorted teddy bear ribbons | (optional) |
| binding | ⅓ yard |
| backing | 1 yard |
| batting | 32" x 45" |

CUTTING GUIDE:

| | |
|---|---|
| A | 11" x 12½" |
| B | 1" x 12½" |
| C | 6½" x 12½" |
| D | 1" x 12½" |
| E | 4½" x 7½" |
| F | 1" x 7½" |
| G | 6" x 8" |
| H | 1" x 6" |
| I | 6" x 6" |
| J | 5" x 8" |
| K | 1" x 8" |
| L | 2½" x 8" |
| M | 6" x 6½" |
| N | 1" x 6" |
| O | 6" x 6" |
| P | 1" x 12½" |
| Q | 2" x 12½" |
| R | 1" x 12½" |
| S | 5" x 7" |
| T | 1" x 7" |
| U | 7" x 8" |
| V | 1" x 14" |
| W | 11½" x 13" |
| X | 1" x 13" |
| Y | 8" x 13" |
| Z | 1" x 13½" |
| AA | 1½" x 14½" |
| BB | 1" x 18½" |
| CC | 2 strips 1" x 26½" |
| DD | 2 strips 1" x 32½" |
| EE | 2 strips 2½" x 32½" |
| FF | 2 strips 2½" x 31½" |
| backing | 34" x 40" |
| binding | 4 strips 1¼" x 44" |

# WE CAN BEARLY WAIT FOR CHRISTMAS

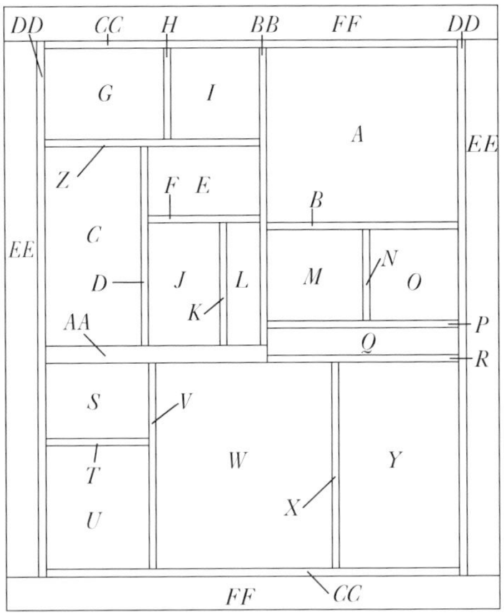


*Figure 7.28—We Can Bearly Wait for Christmas*

*Celia Austin writes: My second quilting class ever, in the fall of 1990, was a memory quilt class. Our assignment was to bring a collection, then design our quilt around it.*

*I started my teddy bear collection about seven years ago with a "mama bear" from Disneyland. I now have more than fifty bears, including stuffed, ceramic, and miniature bears and even bear candles. Most of the year my bears sit on the brass daybed in my sewing room. At Christmastime, I dress several of them in hats, scarves, and mittens and place them on a wooden sled in my entry.*

*The collection I brought to my quilting class included yet more bears assembled over the years—bear fabric, pins, cards, buttons, and ornaments. In my quilt, cloth strips hold the cards in place. The tree block and bear block come from patterns I had saved. A miniature sled and knitted sock adorn other blocks.*

*With three boys, Christmas is very exciting at our home. "We Can Bearly Wait for Christmas" aptly describes our anticipation at that special time of year. Photo 12; finished size, 31½" x 36½".*

## Assembly:

1. To make photo holders for any block, cut two 2½" fabric strips the length and two strips the width of the block. Fold the strips in half lengthwise and press (figure 7.29). Place the horizontal strips on the background blocks, matching raw edges (figure 7.30), then place the vertical strips (figure 7.31) and pin. The raw edges will be sewn into the seams.

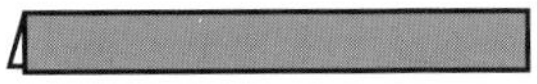

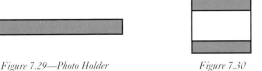

*Figure 7.29—Photo Holder*

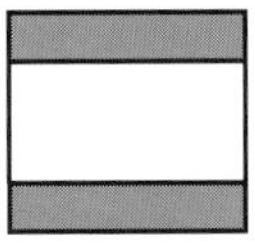

*Figure 7.30*

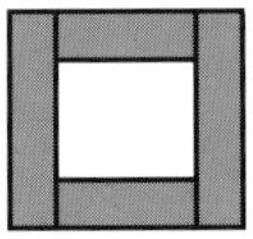

*Figure 7.31*

2. Construct any special blocks like the tree and bear blocks, adding bear ribbon trim as shown or as desired.
3. Assemble the quilt in sections, beginning with smaller sections and adding on (refer to figure 7.28): First, stitch A-B, C-D, and E-F. Next, stitch G-H-I, J-K-L, M-N-O, P-Q-R, S-T-U, and V-W-X-Y.
4. Sew assembled sections together, using strips Z, AA, and BB as indicated.
5. Add borders CC, DD, EE, and finally FF.
6. Layer the quilt and quilt by hand or machine.
7. Stitch the binding strips end to end to make one long strip and bind quilt edges.

# A TOKEN OF FRIENDSHIP

*A collection of gloves started me thinking about a quilt surface for displaying them. As I pondered my gloves and the many hands that wore them, "friendship" came to mind. Near the bottom edge of the quilt are two gloves holding a nosegay. These*

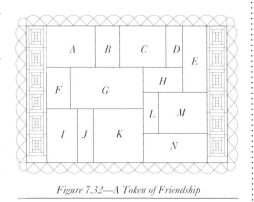

Figure 7.32—A Token of Friendship

*gloves belonged to my daughter, and she passed them on to me. They remind me of when I remarried and she was my maid of honor. The leather glove next to Valori's is one of mine from college, and it holds a hanky given to me by a dear friend. My sister gave me the sheer glove. It is from her mother-in-law, Pearl.*

*Friendship to me means exchanging letters, sending someone a basket of flowers, embroidering a quilt square for a friend. As I worked on the quilt and my friends saw it in progress, they gave me little treasures that found their way onto the quilt. The fabrics and trimmings are part of a collection that you may not be able to duplicate. But once you start on your own version of this quilt, the ideas will flow to you. Look to this quilt for inspiration. Photo, back cover; finished size, 37" x 54".*

## ❦ Assembly:

1. Make the envelope using the pattern on page 89 and following the instructions on page 67, steps 1, 2, 5, and 6.

2. Place the gloves and trims on blocks A–N and tack in place.

3. Stitch the blocks together in sections, then join sections. To join block H, you will need to sew partial seams and come back to complete them as other seams are made. Take your time and try to look ahead.

4. Sew 12 log cabin blocks in the courthouse steps arrangement: From a dark strip, cut twelve 1¼" squares to be the center blocks (1). Following the sequence in figure 7.33, cut and add strips, first lights opposite each other, then darks opposite each other, until the block is complete. Keep alternating lights and darks to produce the step effect. Press after each seam. Block measures 5¾" x 5¾".

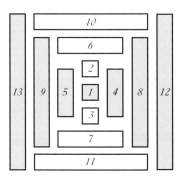

Figure 7.33

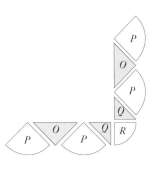

Figure 7.34
Border Placement

## MATERIALS (see figure 7.32):

| | |
|---|---|
| envelope | ¼ yard textured fabric |
| A–N | 1¼ yards total of 14 different floral print fabrics (a different print for each block) |
| log cabin blocks, O, P, Q, R | ¼ yard each of 11 different light and dark satin, taffeta, and moiré fabrics* |
| backing | 2 yards |
| batting | 40" x 57" |

A collection of gloves, hankies, flat lace, ribbons, buttons, and flowers

*To prevent raveling, I backed each with lightweight, woven, fusible interfacing before cutting out.

## CUTTING GUIDE:

As you cut the blocks, lay them in position on a flat surface (or tape or pin to the wall) so you can evaluate the fabrics next to one another.

Patterns O–R are on page 90.

| | |
|---|---|
| A | 10½" x 12½" |
| B | 6½" x 10½" |
| C | 10½" x 12½" |
| D | 4½" x 10½" |
| E | 6½" x 16½" |
| F | 6½" x 10½" |
| G | 10½" x 18½" |
| H | 6½" x 10½" |
| I | 8½" x 13½" |
| J | 4½" x 13½" |
| K | 12½" x 13½" |
| L | 4½" x 10½" |
| M | 10½" x 12½" |
| N | 7½" x 16½" |
| log cabin blocks | 11 strips 1¼" x 45", each from a different fabric. Cut more strips during piecing as you need them. |
| O | 46 |
| P | 50 |
| Q | 8 |
| R | 4 |
| backing | 35" x 51", 5 strips 3½" x 45" |

*Facing for border*

*Figure 7.35*

5. Join log cabin blocks together in two rows of six blocks each. Add an extra strip to the short ends.

6. Make the border strips: Stitch O's and P's together alternately to make two rows of 14 O's and 15 P's each (top and bottom borders) and two rows of 9 O's and 10 P's each (side borders). Sew a Q to each end of top and bottom borders. Sew remaining Q's and R's and attach to side borders (figure 7.34).

7. Add the top and bottom borders, then the side borders, to the quilt.

8. Center the large backing and batting under the quilt top. They will be ½" smaller than the quilt top all the way around—this is fine. Pin the three layers together. Machine-quilt in the ditch on the seams and around the edge of the blocks up to the border.

9. Sew the five backing strips together end to end to make one long strip. From this piece, cut two 56" and two 39" strips.

10. Place the strips on the the quilt border, right sides facing. Be sure to allow the strips to extend past the quilt edge for mitering. Where the strips meet at the corners, turn back the ends on an angle to miter, butt the folds together, and hand-stitch. Trim away excess (figure 7.35).

11. Turn the quilt to the back. Machine-stitch around the edge of the scallops, being careful to pivot exactly where the scallops meet. Clip into the seam at each repeat. Turn and press. This is the facing method of finishing the edge of a quilt. Turn under the edge of the facing and tack to the back of the quilt.

# HANKY MEMORIES

*June Jaegar writes: As a child, I often received hankies from my grandparents and aunt when they returned from trips. The hankies were safely put away in a cedar chest, and I rediscovered them one day. As my plan for a hanky quilt took shape, I realized I didn't have enough of them. My husband remembered that his mother had a hanky collection. She had passed away, but the hankies were found at Grandpa's house. It really worked out nicely having a collection from both sides of the family that I can pass on to my son. One of the hankies is dated 1905. The fan blocks in this quilt were left over from a class that I had taken some time ago. The mood of the blocks and the hankies just seemed to work together. As I started hand quilting the background, I got the idea to add bugle beads. They really add sparkle! Photo 15; finished size, 43" x 54".*

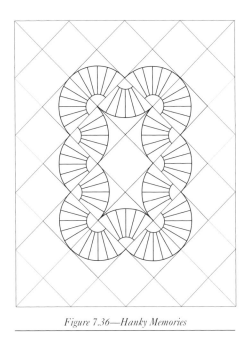

*Figure 7.36—Hanky Memories*

## MATERIALS (see figure 7.36):

| | |
|---|---|
| fabric scraps for fan blades | 2 yards total |
| background fabric | 1¼ yards |
| hankies | 33 to 36 |
| monofilament thread | |
| bugle beads | |
| backing, binding fabric | 1¼ yards |
| batting | 48" x 60" |

## CUTTING GUIDE:

Pattern is on page 93.

| | |
|---|---|
| fan blades | 96 |
| background blocks | 31 blocks 8" x 8"; 9 blocks 8⅞" x 8⅞" (cut in half diagonally for filling in edges) |
| backing | 44" x 58" |
| binding | 5 strips 1¼" x 44" |

## ❦ Assembly:

1. Sew six fan blades together for each block. Press seams in one direction. Make 16 fans.

2. Place each fan on a background block, turn under the top edge of the fan ¼", and appliqué in place.

3. Place a corner of a hanky on the base of each fan. You may want to tuck the hanky at the bottom edge to make it more dimensional. Hand-tack in place or topstitch with monofilament thread.

4. Following figure 7.36, lay out the fan and background blocks. Stitch diagonal rows, using filler triangles at ends. Join the rows.

5. Place the remaining hankies around the edges. Try to take advantage of any definite up-and-down design on a hanky in your arrangement. Topstitch in place with monofilament thread. Trim off the excess (figure 7.37).

6. Layer the quilt. Quilt by hand or machine; this piece was quilted by hand, and beads were worked in.

7. Sew the five binding strips end to end to make one long strip and bind quilt edges.

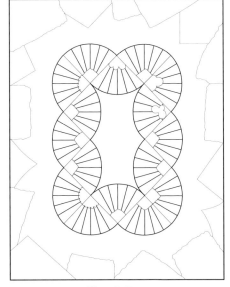

*Figure 7.37*

## MATERIALS
(see figure 7.38 and photo 13):

| | |
|---|---|
| A, D, J, F | ⅓ yard |
| B, H, U, V, letters | ⅓ yard |
| E, K, O | ⅓ yard |
| L | ⅛ yard |
| M | ¼ yard |
| N | ⅛ yard |
| P, R, S, T, backing, | |
| binding | 2⅓ yards |
| Q | ¼ yard |
| solid red fabric | ⅛ yard |
| blue star fabric | 6" x 6" |
| 1" patriotic ribbon | 1⅓ yards |
| assorted charms | 42 |
| 1½" star charms | 5 |
| 1½" x 3" eagle charm | 1 |
| paper-backed | |
| fusible webbing | ½ yard |
| Picture This photo | |
| transfer medium | |
| photographs | |
| batting | 25" x 35" |

## CUTTING GUIDE:

Patterns are on pages 86–89.

| | |
|---|---|
| A | 8" x 10", 8" x 7" |
| | (base for flag appliqué) |
| B | 2½" x 8" |
| C | 7½" x 8½" (photo) |
| D | 2½" x 7½" |
| E | 2½" x 9½" |
| F | 2" x 12½" |
| G | 4" x 6" (photo) |
| H | 3½" x 12½" |
| I | 4 x 5½" (photo) |
| J, K | 2½" x 4" |
| L | 5" x 4" |
| M | 2 |
| N, O, P | 4 (reverse 2) |
| Q | 2 |
| R | 10½" x 21½" |
| | (top will be trimmed |
| | during assembly) |
| S | 9½" x 21½" |
| T | 5¾" x 29" |
| U | 3 (fuse to webbing |
| | before cutting out) |
| V | 4 patriotic print, |
| | 3 blue star fabric |
| | (fuse to webbing |
| | before cutting out) |
| ribbon | six 7½" pieces |
| binding | 3 strips 1¼" x 44" |

# CELEBRATE AMERICA

*Growing up with a father who spent the first two years of my life in a World War II prison camp made me keenly aware of what it means to be an American. My sisters and I knew how precious freedom was and that it didn't come easily. My son joined the army a little over two years ago. When he ended up in the Persian Gulf for Operation Desert Storm, I became even more aware of what my parents went through. I can't even begin to explain the emotions that I felt during his eight-month stay.*

*Sewing has always been my emotional outlet—in bad times as well as good. When I started collecting for this quilt, I found that what I wanted to say was quite personal. This quilt is about my son and what I feel he has contributed to our country. The photographic process proved an easy and wonderful way to transfer his image to fabric. Americana charms add some detail. The quilt took its own shape as it progressed. In working through the themes, I realized that no-sew appliqué using paper-backed fusible webbing was the method I needed to project images like the flag and top banners. This is not a bed quilt that will need repeated washings, so the fusing and photo images will stay intact. My daughter likes it so much that she has put in her request for a senior year quilt about herself! Photo 13; finished size, 22" x 31".*

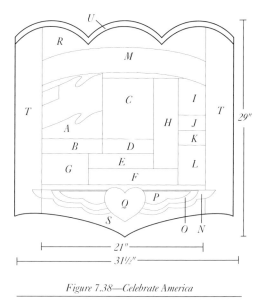

*Figure 7.38—Celebrate America*

❦ Assembly⸵

1. Transfer your photographs from paper to white fabric using Picture This from Plaid Enterprises. Read the directions on the package and follow them carefully. First, make photocopies (black and white or color) of the photographs you wish to use. You can adjust the photocopier to reduce or enlarge the image to the size you need. Allow plenty of time for the chemicals to set up. To help get the paper off the fabric, work a soft brush over it in circular motion, wetting the photo often.

2. Trace patterns for star V and "Celebrate America" letters to paper-backed fusible webbing. Fuse them to their respective fabrics, cut out, then fuse to D, F, J, and M, following photo 15 for placement.

3. To make flag, trace the red stripes to paper-backed webbing. Fuse to the red fabric, cut out, then fuse in position to flag background A. Follow the same procedure with blue star fabric to add blue field. Set aside.

4. Sew interior blocks together in sections: Stitch A to B and C to D, then join these two sections, leaving upper portion of seam A-C open to allow for flag placement. Stitch E to F, stopping ½" from end of E. Stitch G to E-F, then stitch B-D to G-E. Stitch H to C-D-E, then complete F seam. Stitch I, J, K, and L together, then add to F-H edge.

5. Place M, N, O, P, and Q pairs together, right sides facing, and pin to quilt batting. Stitch around the edges, leaving short ends open for turning. Clip the corners and curves. Turn to the right side, press the edges very lightly, and stitch openings shut. The batting gives these pieces extra dimension.

6. On a flat surface, lay out pieced interior and position R above it. Referring to photo 15, place flag on A, with raw side edges aligned and top right corner extending above A. Place M on R, overlapping flag corner. Once you have adjusted the placement, remove M and set aside. Slip a few small pieces of fusible webbing behind the flag and fuse down.

7. Complete the A-C seam, catching in flag as you sew. Sew R to C-H-I edge, stopping at flag. Clip seam, then tuck R behind flag. Add more webbing behind flag and fuse it securely to A and R.

8. Write personal or historical information on blocks A, D, and J with a permanent fabric pen, available at most quilt shops.

9. To shape the bottom edge of S, fold the fabric in half crosswise with folded edge on the right. Measure down 6" from top left and mark. Using a ruler and marking pencil, draw a line connecting this mark to the lower right corner (folded edge). Using this line as a guide, draw a gently curving arch across S (figure 7.39).Trim off excess fabric.

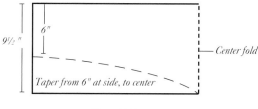

9½"

6"

Center fold

Taper from 6" at side, to center

*Figure 7.39*

10. Sew S to G-F-L at the bottom of the quilt. Sew T's to each side of the quilt.

11. Fuse the three U's to the top edge of the quilt. Trim quilt to match U curves, leaving a ¼" allowance to be covered by binding

12. Trace star quilting patterns W and X randomly on the sides of the quilt. Layer the quilt. Stitch in the ditch between the blocks. Quilt the stars by hand or machine.

13. Place M on quilt with six cut ribbons just under the ends (see photo 13). Tack the underside of M to the top of the quilt. Tack the ribbons in place. Sew charms to the lower edge of U.

14. Layer N, O, P, and Q on quilt (see photo 13) and tack in place.

15. Stitch the three binding strips end to end to make one long strip and bind the quilt edges.

MATERIALS (see figure 7.40):

background fabric
    for blocks A–G    1¼ yards
        sky fabric    ½ yard
    water fabric    ¼ yard
sashing, borders    1 yard
assorted scraps for appliqué
black six-strand embroidery floss for vehicles
and tugboat
embellishments for treasure chest
        backing    1½ yards
Thermolam fleece    1½ yards
  collection of keys
        frame    (optional, depending
                on weight of
                collection)

## CUTTING GUIDE:

| | | |
|---|---|---|
| A | 14½" x 12" | |
| B, C | 10½" x 12" | |
| D | 14½" x 12" | |
| E | 9½" x 12" | |
| F | 42½" x 12" | |
| G | 4½" x 53½" | |
| sashing | 4 strips 1½" x 44" | |
| | plus 4 bias strips | |
| | 2" x 15" (for curved | |
| | pieces on blocks A, | |
| | D, and F; optional) | |
| borders | 5 strips 4½" x 44" | |
| | (includes 2" to 2½" | |
| | allowance for | |
| | framing) | |

# CAROLYN'S KEYS

*Marrell Dickson writes: My sister Carolyn has always collected keys. She is especially fond of her jail key, the keys that go to a tugboat, and the hotel key from London, carried home by our father, who served in the Air Corps during World War II. Some of the keys, like the one to the castle, were originally made for decoration.*

*Although I put a good amount of thought into the quilt before I received the keys, most of the block designs came to me after seeing the keys firsthand and talking with Carolyn. At first I had problems deciding what to do with the jail key, but one day when I was telling someone about the quilt "The Untimely Demise of*

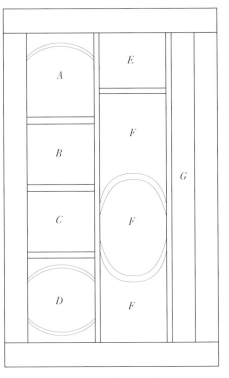

*Figure 7.40—Carolyn's Keys*

*Sunbonnet Sue," I decided I just couldn't resist a jailbreak. I kept the blocks simple throughout, and my husband even got involved sketching the cars. He reminded me that for years Carolyn drove a '65 Chevy van that was unique—yellow with a blue stripe. The other car somehow ended up shaped like mine.*

*This quilt should be viewed up close in order to take in the detail. Making it was a very fulfilling experience for me. I made decisions by relating everything back to Carolyn, trying to remember what she had said when we discussed the collection. Machine quilting made the surface come alive. Photo 30; frame opening measures 34" x 57".*

❧ Assembly:

Because of the personal nature of the keys and their relationship to the block content, only general instructions will be given for the quilt block designs. The content of your blocks can and should be different! Keep an eye out for patterns that mean something personal to you, or create your own. Patterns, too, can become part of your collection.

1. Appliqué the individual blocks as desired. The heart pattern in block C is from *A Celebration of Hearts* by Jean Wells and Marina Anderson. The castle in block G is a variation of "Churches," from Georgia Bonesteel's *Spools, Spools, Spools.* To "frame" your designs with arcs, as shown on blocks A, D, and F, position the bias strips on the blocks, turn under edges ¼", and appliqué in place.

2. Join blocks with sashing, short strips first, then long strips. Add G at right edge.

3. Stitch three of the border strips together end to end to make one long strip. From this piece, cut two 51½" strips and add to quilt sides. Cut the two remaining strips to 37½" and add to quilt top and bottom.

4. Layer the quilt, and quilt by hand or machine. Tack the keys to the surface with heavy thread. Frame, then glue additional keys to the frame.

# CLOTHING

*Yardages are for adult sizes 10 and 12 and girl's size 4. If you are making a smaller or larger size, vary the yardage accordingly.*

❦

## ❦ Layered Appliqué

Layered appliqué can be worked into the design of many commercial patterns—just give your creativity free reign. See chapter 3 for detailed instructions on layered appliqué collage and chapters 4 and 5 for tips on working with ribbons and buttons. Once the layered appliqué is in place, complete the garment according to the instructions in the commercial pattern. You can also work directly on purchased clothing. Keep in mind that your laces do not need to look exactly like the ones in the photos to be beautiful!

## WHITE-ON-WHITE BLOUSE

*Only two main pattern pieces—front and back—are needed for this simple blouse with dainty sleeves. The pattern I used included a flap at the front that concealed the buttons—perfect for appliqué. Photo 4.*

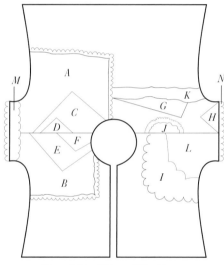

*Figure 7.41—White on White Blouse*

MATERIALS (see figure 7.41):

commercial blouse pattern with 2 main pattern pieces

| | |
|---|---|
| A, B | 2 lace-edged place mats |
| C, D, E, F, G, H, I | three 12" hankies or napkins |
| J | 8" doily |
| K, M | ½ yard flat 2" lace |
| L | napkin |
| N | ⅔ yard flat 1" lace |

monofilament thread

## ❦ Cutting and assembly:

1. Cut out the blouse pieces according to the pattern instructions.

2. Cut and position lace appliqués as shown in figure 7.41 or as desired. I appliquéd laces A–K to the front and back pattern pieces before doing any of the blouse construction. Then I sewed the shoulder seams and added laces L and M across the sleeves.

3. Sew the blouse according to the pattern instructions.

# ANTIQUE LACE BLOUSE

*This blouse pattern features a plain front, stand-up collar, and back opening. The background fabric is linen. Photo 9.*

MATERIALS (see figure 7.42):

commercial long-sleeved blouse pattern with simple lines

| | |
|---|---|
| linen for bodice | 1½ yards |
| print fabric for sleeves | ¾ yard |
| A | corner of a tablecloth |
| B | 10" doily |
| C | 1" flat lace, ⅓ yard |
| D | 1¼" flat lace, ½ yard |
| E | napkin |
| F | ¼" lace, ⅓ yard |
| G | 1¼" flat lace, ½ yard |
| H | 5" doily |
| I | ¾" flat lace, ¼ yard |
| J | ½" flat lace, ¼ yard |
| narrow cording | ⅓ yard |
| narrow ribbons | ½ yard each three different colors |
| narrow ribbon garland (optional) | ⅓ yard |
| assorted buttons | |
| ¼" to ⅝" | 14 |
| ¼" buttons | 10 |
| ¼" buttons | 5 (can be different) |
| small ribbon roses | 5 |
| monofilament thread | |

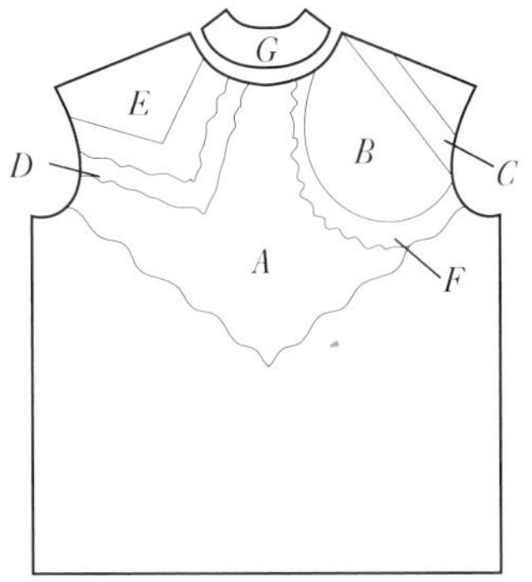


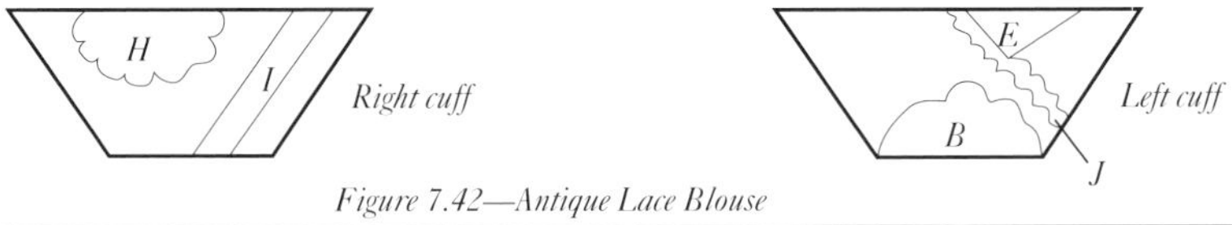


*Figure 7.42—Antique Lace Blouse*

## ❦ Cutting and assembly:

1. Cut out the blouse pieces according to the pattern instructions.
2. Place the tablecloth corner A on the center front of the blouse bodice, and add appliqués B–F.
3. Embellish with ribbons and buttons. I put two colors of narrow ribbon on doily B, twisting and turning it and securing it with buttons. I sewed small buttons under lace D. I tacked narrow cording, buttons, and tiny ribbon loops to napkin E and tiny ribbon roses to lace F.
4. Add appliqué G to collar and appliqués B, E, H, I, and J to cuffs. I worked a row of doodle quilting on the collar under lace G. On the right cuff, I tacked two narrow ribbons to lace I and worked doodle quilting around the edge of doily H. On the left cuff, I echoed the same two ribbons on doily B and worked doodle quilting along the edge of lace J.
5. Assemble the blouse according to the pattern instructions.

# LITTLE GIRL'S DRESS BODICE

*Little girl's dresses are my favorite garments to decorate and try new ideas. The size of a little dress is similar to that of a small pillow—you'll find yourself scaling down the design. Photo 10.*

MATERIALS (see figure 7.43):

commercial dress pattern with plain bodice or yoke
dresser scarf large enough for bodice pattern

| | |
|---|---|
| A | 5" doily with a lace edge |
| B | 6" lace doily |
| C | three 2½" crocheted or tatted doilies or lace appliqués |
| D | flat lace 2½" x 5" |
| E | flat lace 1¼" x 8" |
| F | flat lace 1½" x 7" |
| 1½" ribbon | ¼ yard (place under D) |
| 1½" ribbon | ¼ yard (place under E) |
| ⅜" ribbon | 2 pieces ¼ yard each (place alongside B) |
| ¾" buttons | 3 |
| assorted buttons | |
| ½" or smaller | 30 |
| monofilament thread | |

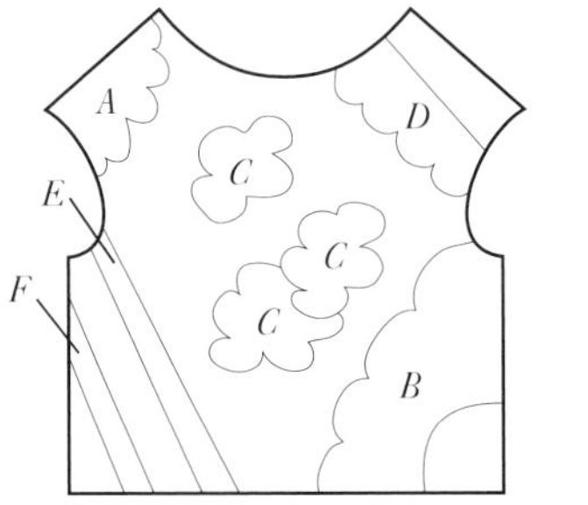


*Figure 7.43—Little Girl's Dress Bodice*

## ❦ Cutting and assembly:

1. Cut the front bodice from the dresser scarf.
2. Referring to figure 7.43 for placement ideas, layer on lace appliqués A–F. Add 1½" ribbons under laces D and E to add a little color. Tack laces and ribbons by hand or machine-stitch the edges with monofilament thread.
3. Embellish with buttons and ribbons. I placed the three ¾" buttons on lace E and the smaller buttons on and below lace D and on doilies A and C. I arranged two pieces of ⅜" ribbon on doily B, clustering buttons on top.
4. Fill in the empty spaces with doodle quilting (page 24) to enhance the design.
5. Cut and sew the remaining pattern pieces from the fabric of your choice and assemble with the bodice following the pattern instructions.

# LITTLE GIRL'S COLLAR

*This fresh rose print in pink and green reminded me of a little girl. The collar picks up on the colors with some green crocheted lace and a tea towel with some green in it. The little tatted pink circles were a find at a sale. A large damask napkin was used for the background. Photo 8.*

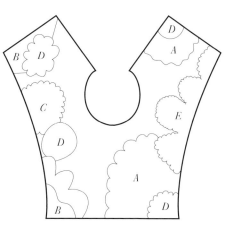

*Figure 7.44—Little Girl's Collar*

MATERIALS (see figure 7.44):

commercial dress pattern with a
detachable collar
22"-square damask dinner napkin
fabric for lining collar
| | | |
|---|---|---|
| A | 4" fabric doily | |
| B | tea towel with a lace edge | |
| C | 3" tatted doily | |
| D | three 2" tatted doilies | |
| E | 2" flat lace, ¼ yard | |
| 1¼" flat lace to edge collar | ¾ yard | |
| ⅛" satin ribbon | ½ yard | |
| 1" buttons | 3 | |
| ¼" buttons in a variety of shapes | 27 | |
| monofilament thread | | |

❦ **Cutting and assembly:**

1. Cut one collar from the large dinner napkin and one from the lining.

2. Referring to figure 7.44, place the appliqués on the collar. Tack the lace in place by hand or machine-stitch the edges with monofilament thread.

3. Embellish with buttons and ribbons. I sewed the large buttons to the three D doilies. I tacked a smaller button to doily C, slipping a small ribbon loop underneath it. The remaining ribbon is placed under lace E and loops and twists across tea towel B. The remaining buttons are sewn to doily A, the top D doily, and tea towel B.

4. Add quilting. I worked doodle quilting in the open spaces between the laces as a decorative filler.

# APPLIQUÉD DENIM JACKET

*This purchased denim jacket caught my eye because it was collarless—it just screamed for embellishment! First, I fused on sections cut from a large floral print. I had started carrying packages of plastic rhinestones and pearls in my retail store, and I was sure that if I showed them in a sample garment, they would sell better. I love pink and green and the crispness of the white laces with the denim. Photos 20 and 21.*

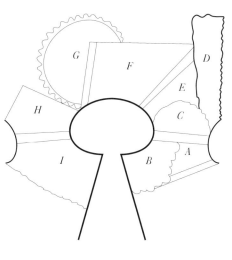

*Figure 7.45—Appliquéd Denim Jacket*

MATERIALS (see figure 7.45):

purchased denim jacket, preferably without
collar (or remove collar)
| | | |
|---|---|---|
| A | ¼ yard large floral print fabric | |
| B, D, E, F, I | 2 white place mats with Battenberg lace edging | |
| C | 8" doily | |
| G | 10" doily | |
| H | hanky | |
| 1½" ribbon | ⅔ yard | |
| ⅝" ribbon | ⅓ yard | |
| roses | 3 medium large, 2 medium, 1 small | |
| pearls | | |
| plastic rhinestones | | |
| ⅜" ribbon | 2 yards | |
| ¼" ribbon | ½ yard | |
| ⅛" ribbon | 1 yard | |
| ⅜" flat braid | 1 yard | |
| paper-backed fusible webbing | ½ yard | |
| monofilament thread | | |

❦ **Cutting and assembly:**

1. Referring to figure 7.45, layer on appliqués A–H. Butt pieces up against one another (you'll cover raw edges with ribbon later), and stitch with monofilament thread.

2. Cut an appropriately sized floral design from fabric and fuse to I and F.

3. Cover raw edges with ribbon: Sew ⅝" ribbon on outer edge of B and on F-G and E-F. Sew 1½" ribbon on AB-C and H-I.

4. Referring to photos 20 and 21, shape remaining ribbons into bows and loops and sew on with roses, pearls, and rhinestones.

5. Sew ⅜" flat braid around neckline.

MATERIALS (see figure 7.46):

commercial vest pattern with simple lines, few interior seams

| | |
|---|---|
| A, back | ¾ yard |
| B, C | ⅔ yard each |
| lining | ¾ yard |
| muslin or flannel foundation | ¾ yard |
| lace collars or doilies for inserts | 2 |
| 2" flat lace for seam BC insert | ⅓ yard |
| 1" flat lace for seam BC insert | 1⅓ yards |
| narrow decorative cording | 2 yards |
| charms | approximately 50 (a different arrangement might take less) |

## CHARM VEST

*Simple curved piecing with lace inserts makes this vest the perfect backdrop for charms. The background fabrics are moiré, and the inserts are pieces of collars and flat lace. With charms so collectable, why not display them on a garment? Photo 32.*

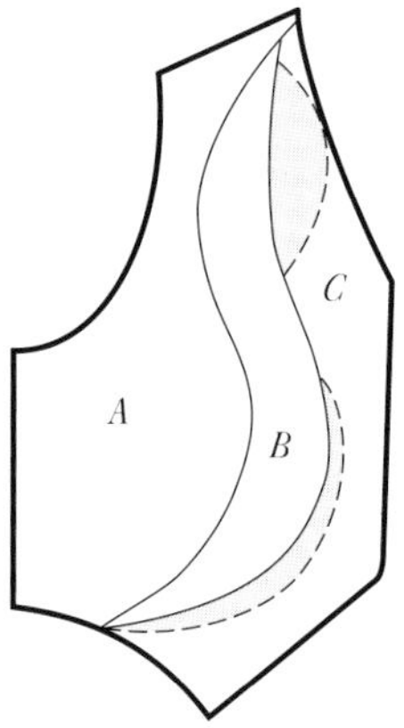


*Figure 7.46—Charm Vest*

### ❦ Cutting and assembly:

1. Following the instructions on pages 22–23 and referring to figure 7.46, make three curved piecing patterns for the vest front.

2. Cut out all curved pieces, vest back, foundation, and lining from selected fabrics. Remember to add seam allowances to curved pieces (page 22, step 8).

3. Sew curved pieces together (page 23, steps 12–15), inserting lace doily sections in the seams before stitching.

4. Hand-sew the cording to seam BC, forming a small circle every 2"–3". The circles will look like small loops.

5. Complete the vest, including the lining, following the pattern instructions. Hand-sew the charms to the cording.

MATERIALS (see figure 7.47):

commercial vest pattern with traditional styling (points at lower front)

| | |
|---|---|
| back, lining, pocket flap fabric | 1½ yards |
| muslin or flannel foundation fabric | ¾ yard |
| 5 different fabrics for piecing and pocket flap | ¼ yard each |
| 1½" flat lace for seam BC insert | ¼ yard |
| 2½" flat lace for GF, H, IJ, and K seam inserts | 1 yard |
| narrow cording | 2½ yards |
| ½" flat braid for pocket flaps | ½ yard |
| 1" ribbon | 1 yard |
| ⅝" ribbon | 1½ yards |
| 2 different ⅛" ribbons | 1 yard each |
| charms | 3 |
| buttons, ¼" to 1" | 80 to 100 |

## BUTTON-ADORNED VEST

*A white blouse with brass buttons sewn on the collar inspired this vest. When I bought the blouse, my mind simply raced with ideas for a vest to go with it. I ended up strip-piecing several different kinds of black fabric as a backdrop for my collection of buttons, ribbons, charms, and lace. A purchased heart pin provides a focal point. The vest is heavy to wear with all the buttons but a great showpiece. Photo 1.*

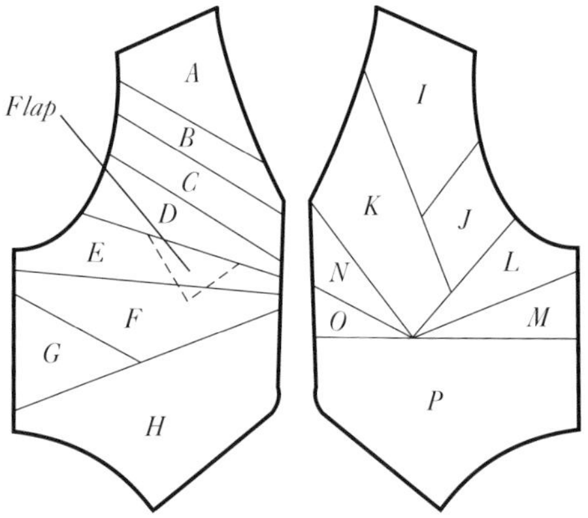


*Figure 7.47—Button-Adorned Vest*

### ❦ Cutting and assembly:

1. Trace two vest fronts onto tracing paper (reverse one). Referring to figure 7.47, use a ruler to draw lines on each pattern to create sections for piecing. Notch each seamline and label each section as you do for curved piecing (page 22, steps 4 and 5).

2. Cut the pattern pieces apart. Determine where you want each fabric in the patchwork scheme. Pin the pattern pieces on the right side of the chosen fabric and cut out, adding ¼" seam allowance to all notched edges (the seam allowance is

already included in the outer edges). With a marking pencil, draw a dot on the fabric seamline to mark the notch (figure 7.48).

3. Cut vest back, lining, and pocket flap (pattern is on page 81) from the main fabric. Cut vest fronts and back from the foundation fabric.

4. Starting with the right front, stitch the patchwork pieces to the foundation. Lay A in place at the shoulder. Place B on A, right sides facing, raw edges even, and dots matching (figure 7.49). Stitch ¼" from raw edge through the three layers of fabric. Flip B to the right side. This method is like strip piecing or quilt-as-you-go. Stitching through the foundation creates a raised effect that looks like quilting.

5. Place any lace inserts on the piece just sewn before the next strip is added. The raw edges will be enclosed in the seam (figure 7.50).

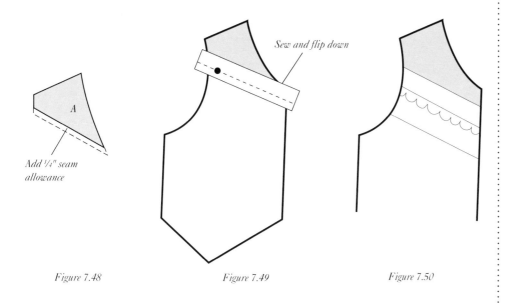

*Add ¼" seam allowance*

*Sew and flip down*

Figure 7.48                     Figure 7.49                     Figure 7.50

6. Continue to D. To make the inset flap, cut one pocket from piecing fabric. Place on pocket lining, right sides facing, and stitch along two shorter edges. Clip the corners and point. Turn to right side and press. Sew ½" flat braid to edges.

7. Place the right side of the flap on the raw edge of D. Place E on top, matching the dots as above, and stitch seam. Press flap down and tack if necessary. Continue adding pieces F–H until the right vest front foundation is covered. Sew pieces I–P to left front in same way.

8. Look closely at photo 1 for ideas for the ribbon, cording, and button placement. I started by tacking cording over the seams, letting it swirl and flow like doodle quilting. I added lace to the seam edges. I spaced the most interesting buttons across the vest fronts, then filled in with ribbon loops and the more ordinary buttons.

9. Complete the vest following pattern instructions. Layer the back foundation between the linings for extra body.

## ADULT'S COLLAR MATERIALS:

| | |
|---|---|
| white cotton fabric | ½ yard |
| flat, dense batting | 18" x 18" |
| white cotton thread | |
| for appliqué | 2 small spools or 1 large spool |

## CHILD'S COLLAR MATERIALS:

| | |
|---|---|
| white cotton fabric | ½ yard |
| flat, dense batting | 15" x 30" |
| white cotton thread | |
| for appliqué | 2 small spools or 1 large spool |

## HANDBAG MATERIALS:

| | |
|---|---|
| white cotton fabric | |
| (outside and lining) | ¾ yard |
| flat, dense batting | 17" x 20" |
| white cotton thread | |
| for appliqué | 1½ small spools or 1 large spool |

## MATERIALS:

| | |
|---|---|
| fabric | ¼ yard |
| 2" nonroll elastic | your waist measurement less 2" |
| Velcro | 2" |
| posterboard | 2 pieces 2" x 4" |
| thin batting | 2" x 4" |
| ⅛" ribbon | 1 yard |
| 1" novelty buttons | 7 |
| ⅛" novelty buttons | 5 |
| shirt buttons, | |
| ¼" to ⅛" | 40 |
| Tacky glue or a hot glue gun | |

# QUILTED LACE

*Here are three projects featuring Miranda Stewart's quilted lace technique. The collars are detachable and could circle a dress or sweater neckline. The handbag is a basic envelope pattern with quilted lace on the flap. The patterns (pages 90–91) must be enlarged on a photocopy machine as indicated. Yardage amounts are given at left. Once you have enlarged the pattern and collected the yardage, turn to the quilted lace instructions on page 16. Photos 2 and 3.*

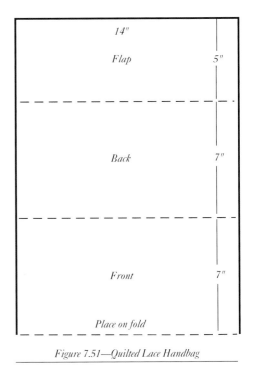

*Figure 7.51—Quilted Lace Handbag*

### ❧ Cutting and assembly for handbag:

Referring to figure 7.51, fold whole fabric in half and cut outer envelope and lining in one piece. Assemble as for layered lace pillow (page 67, steps 2, 5, and 6), then work quilted lace on flap.

# ADORNMENTS

# BUTTON BELT BUCKLES

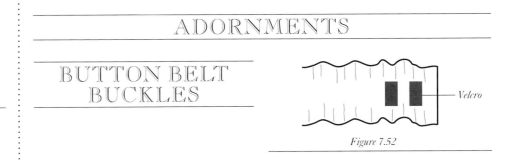

*Figure 7.52*

*Loops of ribbon and a variety of buttons are stitched to fabric, then wrapped over cardboard to make these decorative belt buckles. The buckle is 2" x 4" and the belt is 2" wide. You can easily adjust belt length shorter or longer. Photos 22, 23, and 25.*

### ❧ Cutting and assembly:

1. Cut a 5" x 45" fabric strip. Fold lengthwise, right sides facing, and stitch long raw edges. Turn right side out and press.

2. Using a safety pin, thread the elastic through the fabric. Stitch across the ends of the belt through both fabric and elastic.

3. Cut Velcro into two 1" pieces and separate it. Place the two "loop" Velcro pieces on one end of the belt, ¼" apart, and topstitch in place (figure 7.52). (continued on page 65)

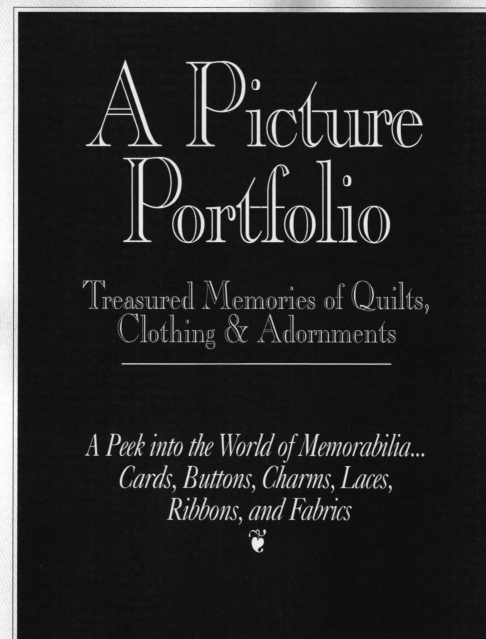

# A Picture Portfolio

Treasured Memories of Quilts,
Clothing & Adornments

*A Peek into the World of Memorabilia...
Cards, Buttons, Charms, Laces,
Ribbons, and Fabrics*

Photo 1
Button-Adorned
Vest

Photo 2
Quilted Lace Handbag

Photo 3
Quilted Lace Collars

Photo 4
White~on~White
Blouse

Photo 5
Fantasy Basket
Pillow

Photo 6
Layered Lace
Envelope Pillow

51

Photo 7
Fantasy Basket Quilt

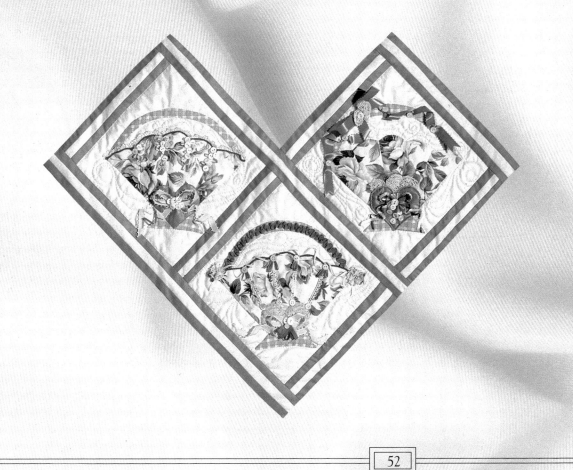

Photo 9
Antique Lace Blouse

Photo 8
Little Girl's Collar

Photo 10
Little Girl's Dress Bodice

LAYERED
APPLIQUÉ

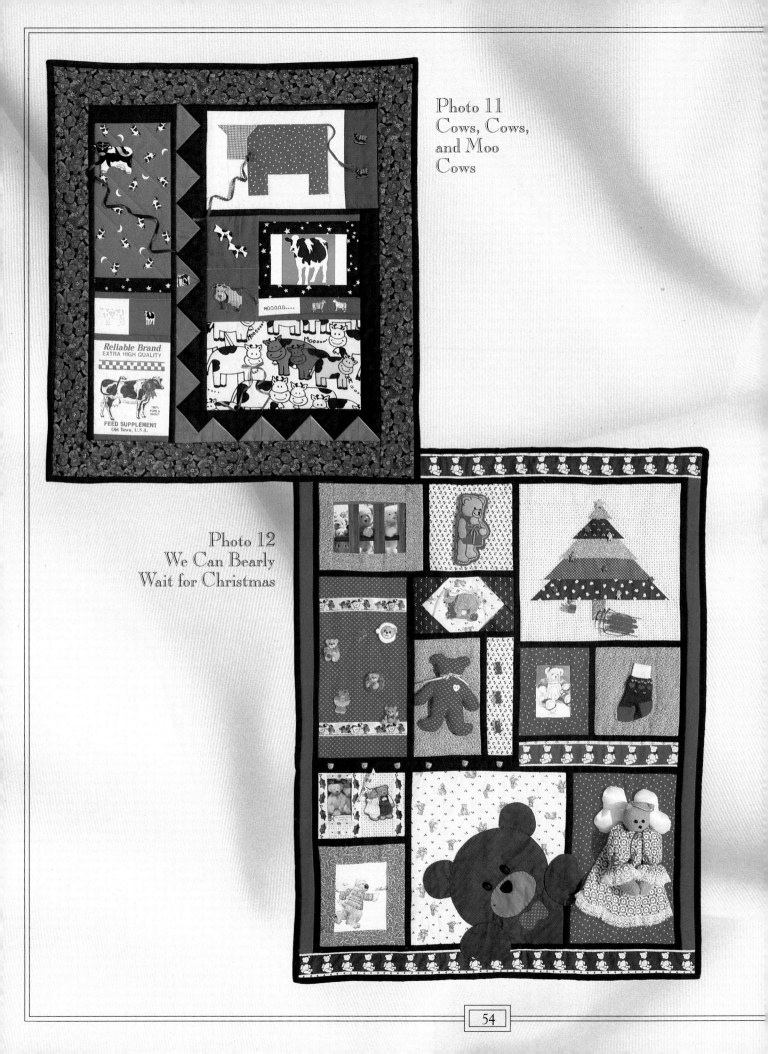

Photo 11
Cows, Cows,
and Moo
Cows

Photo 12
We Can Bearly
Wait for Christmas

Photo 13    Celebrate America

Photo 14
Portrait Holder

Photo 15
Hanky Memories

Photo 16
Quilter's Caddy

Photo 17
Framed Doll Collage

Photo 18
Framed Memorabilia Collage

Photo 19
Portable Desk

**Photo 20
Layered Appliqué
Jacket (Back)**

**Photo 21
Layered Appliqué Jacket
(Front)**

**Photo 22
Button-Embellished Belt Buckle
& Brooches**

**Photo 23
Button-Embellished Brooches,
Belt & Bracelet**

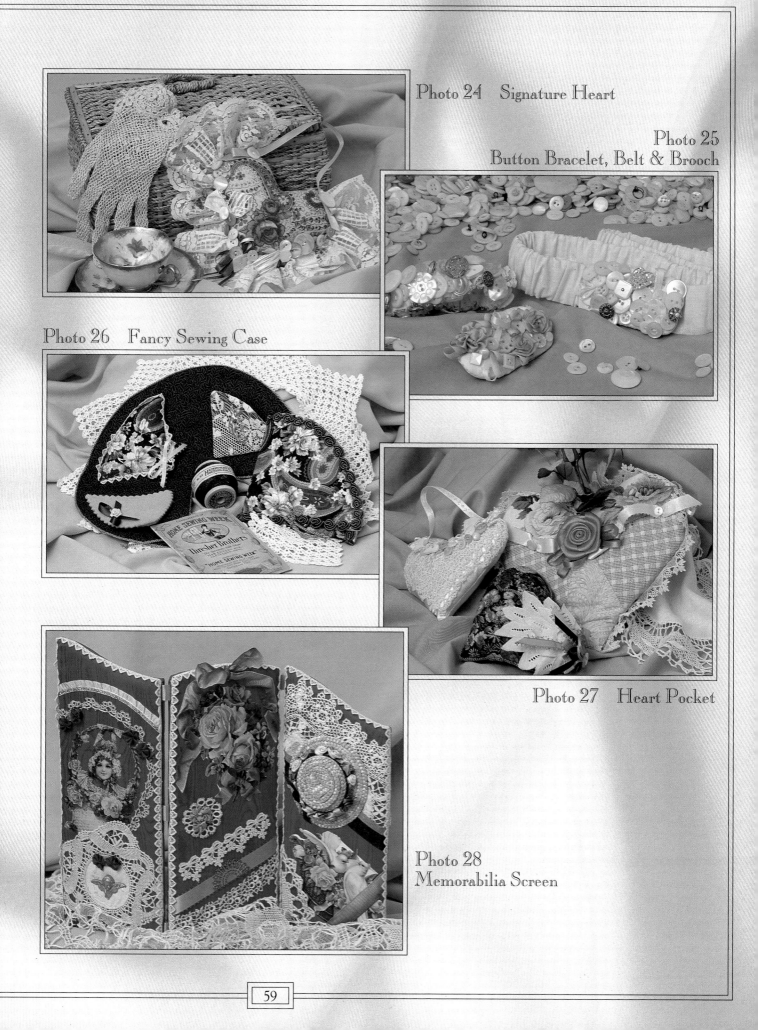

Photo 24   Signature Heart

Photo 25
Button Bracelet, Belt & Brooch

Photo 26   Fancy Sewing Case

Photo 27   Heart Pocket

Photo 28
Memorabilia Screen

Photo 29
Four-Block Sampler

Photo 30
Carolyn's Keys

Photo 31
Heart Button
Collection

Photo 32
Charm Vest

Photo 33
Heart Pocket

Photo 34
Rosy Yellow

Photo 35
Heart Pocket

Photo 36    A Portrait of Hearts

Photo 37    Evening Sky

4. Round the corners of the posterboard and batting. Place posterboard template on wrong side of fabric and lightly trace outline. Cut out fabric ⅜" beyond marked line. Repeat to cut second buckle.

   5. Center the batting behind one of the pieces of fabric. Sew on all the buttons through the fabric and batting, keeping inside the pencil lines. Start with some of the ordinary buttons—they will be the backdrop for the more interesting buttons. Layer buttons as you go. Add ribbon loops, then complete final layer of buttons.

   6. Place the posterboard behind the fabric-button piece and pull the raw edges of the fabric to the back. Glue the edges to the posterboard (figure 7.53a). Repeat to cover the other piece of posterboard.

   7. Place the two pieces together, inserting the belt end without the Velcro ¼" inside. Hand-stitch the belt in place, then sew around the edges. Sew the remaining Velcro halves to the back of the belt buckle (figure 7.53b).

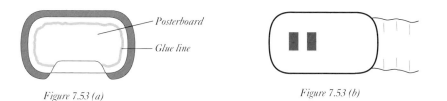

*Figure 7.53 (a)*                    *Figure 7.53 (b)*

## BUTTON BROOCHES

*Button brooches are made just like the button belt buckles. The cardboard shapes can be rectangular, square, oval, round, triangular, or heart-shaped. The amount of buttons needed depends upon the size and shape of the brooch and the size buttons you choose. Ribbon loops and ribbon roses make nice fill-ins. Once the cardboard shape is determined, cut it out and proceed as for the buckle, steps 4–6. Sew the halves together and stitch a pin to the back. Photos 22, 23, and 25.*

## BUTTON BRACELETS

*A variety of buttons are stitched to an elasticized ribbon for this novelty bracelet. Depending on the character of your buttons, the look can vary from elegant to casual. When I was little, my Grandma Tot crocheted button bracelets for me with gold elastic thread. Photos 23 and 25.*

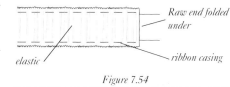

*Figure 7.54*

**❦ Cutting and assembly:**

   1. Cut the ribbon in half crosswise for two 18" lengths. Fold each short end ¼" to the inside and press. Place the two ribbons together, edges matching and folds concealed. Topstitch along each side close to the edge (figure 7.54).

   2. Using a safety pin, pull the elastic through the ribbon casing. Overlap the ends of the elastic ¼" and stitch. Smooth the ends of the ribbon over the seam so that they meet and stitch together.

   3. Sew on the buttons in layers, as for the belt buckle, starting with the ordinary ones and working up to the novelty ones.

**MATERIALS:**

| | |
|---|---|
| ¾" elastic | 8" |
| 1" grosgrain ribbon | 1 yard |
| 1" novelty buttons | 7 |
| ⅜" novelty buttons | 8 |
| shirt buttons, ⅛" to ⅞" | 35 |

MATERIALS:

| | |
|---|---|
| case fabric | ⅓ yard |
| lining fabric | ⅓ yard |
| contrast fabric or lace for pocket | ⅛ yard |
| flannel for filling | ⅓ yard |
| narrow cord for trim and ties (optional for inside pocket) | 2 yards |
| flat narrow lace to trim pincushion | ⅜ yard |
| felt for needlecase | |
| ¼" ribbon for bow on needlecase | ¼ yard |
| fiberfill | small amount for pincushion |

*This soft fabric sewing case is complete with pincushion, thimble holder, and needlecase. It makes a great gift for a friend—or make one for yourself to carry with you. Closed and tied, the case forms a fan shape. When opened, sewing tools are at your fingertips. Photo 26; finished size, 5" x 5".*

❦ Cutting and assembly:

Patterns are on page 93.

1. Trace pattern A three times, arranging in a "pie" for one large pattern. Use the pattern to cut one case, one lining, and one flannel filling, adding ¼" seam allowance on straight edges (figure 7.55).

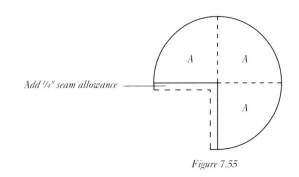

*Figure 7.55*

2. Place case and lining together, right sides facing. Place on flannel. Stitch around the edges, leaving 3" opening along a straight edge for turning. Clip the corners and clip into the point. Turn.

3. From case fabric, cut 4 of pattern B for pincushion and pocket. From felt, cut 3 B for needlecase, trimming away seam allowance on all edges.

4. For pincushion, place two B's together, right sides facing, and stitch, leaving an opening for turning. Clip the corners, turn to the right side, and stuff. Add lace around the edge. Stitch to the middle fan section of the sewing case.

5. For pocket, follow step 4, but do not stuff. Hand-sew the pocket to the right fan section, manipulating so a thimble can fit in it. Add cording by hand if you wish.

6. For needlecase, make a ribbon bow and tack to the layered felt. Attach to the left fan section.

# LAYERED LACE ENVELOPE PILLOW

*The flap on a fabric envelope is a great place to feature collected memorabilia. Possibly you've found doilies with stained or torn edges. You can feature the good part on a small section of the flap. When a pillow form is slipped inside, the envelope becomes a cushion. Photo 6.*

❧ Cutting and assembly:

1. Referring to figure 7.56, cut outer envelope and lining.

2. Place envelope right side down on a flat surface, with flap at the bottom. Measuring from the flap edge, mark and fold on lines indicated. Press.

3. Referring to figure 7.57, decorate the flap: Place doilies A and C and collars B and D on the flap and tack in place.

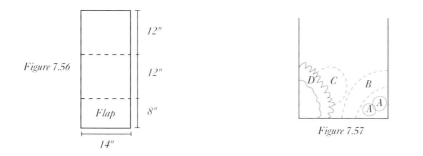

*Figure 7.56*

12"

12"

*Flap* 8"

14"

*Figure 7.57*

4. Embellish with button and ribbons: I looped and twisted the ⅜" ribbon along the edges of collars B and D, then added buttons in clusters. I also sewed buttons to doily C.

5. Place envelope and lining together, rights sides facing. Stitch the short end opposite the flap and around the flap, backtacking at the fold line at each side. Clip to the stitching line (figure 7.58). Also clip corners. Turn to the right side and press.

6. With flap at top, fold bottom edge up, lining side out, to form pocket. Stitch sides (figure 7.59). Clip corners, turn, and press.

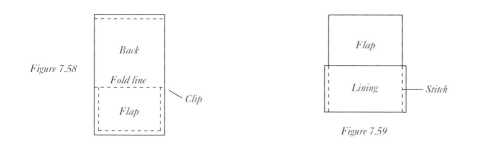

*Figure 7.58*

*Back*

*Fold line*

*Flap*

— *Clip*

*Flap*

*Lining* — *Stitch*

*Figure 7.59*

7. Hand-sew flat lace to the flap edge, making a tuck at each corner to keep the lace flat.

8. For pillow insert, measure the envelope pouch and add ½" seam allowance all around. Cut two pieces of fabric to this measurement. Place together, right sides facing, and sew with a ½" seam allowance, leaving a 3" opening for turning. Clip the corners, turn, press, and stuff. Insert into pillow envelope.

MATERIALS (see figure 7.57):

| | |
|---|---|
| outer envelope fabric | ⅜ yard |
| envelope lining and pillow fabric | ⅝ yard |
| A | two 3" doilies |
| B, D | 2 lace collar halves |
| C | 6" doily |
| buttons, ⅞" or smaller | 40 |
| ⅛" feather-edge ribbon | 1 yard |
| 1½" flat lace for edge of flap | 1 yard |
| fiberfill | about 10 oz. |

## MATERIALS (see figure 7.60):

| | |
|---|---|
| A, B, C, G | ¼ yard |
| D, F | 7" x 10" |
| H, backing | ½ yard |
| I, J, K | ⅛ yard |
| L, M | ⅛ yard |
| Thermolam fleece | ½ yard |
| fiberfill | about 12 oz. |
| 1½" ribbon | 1 yard |
| large flower | (this one was purchased) |
| ⅝" ribbon | ⅔ yard |
| ⅛" ribbon | 3¼ yards |
| narrow cording | 1½ yards |

## CUTTING GUIDE:

Patterns A, B, C, D, and F are on page 80; G is on page 77; E is not used.

| | |
|---|---|
| A | 2 (reverse 1) |
| B | 2 |
| C | 1 |
| D | 1 |
| F | 1 |
| G | 10 |
| H | 10½" x 13½" |
| I | 3½" x 13½" |
| J | 2 strips 1½" x 13½" |
| K | 1½" x 15½" |
| L | 2½" x 15½" |
| M | 2½" x 16½" |
| backing | 16½" x 19½" |
| Thermolam fleece | 16½" x 19½" |

# FANTASY BASKET PILLOW

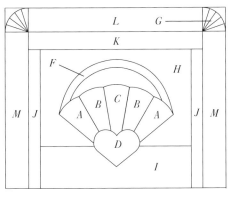

*Figure 7.60—Fantasy Basket Pillow*

*This pillow project shows how you can vary a basic quilt block pattern and add borders to create a different image. Look closely and you'll recognize the basic block from "Fantasy Basket" (photo 7). I left off the stand on each side of the basket and let the heart shape drop down into the border. The border is asymmetrical, showing smaller pieced fans at the top edge only. The ribbon design in the blue fabric gave me the idea for sewing tiny bows on the basket handle. To repeat the ribbon theme, I quilted ribbons in the background and added ribbons to the border. The border is finished with a flange edge on three sides. Photo 5; finished size, 15" x 15".*

### ❦ Assembly:

1. Sew A's, B's, and C together to make basket, ending with a tack stitch ¼" from the top (curved) edge. Press seams open.

2. Referring to figure 7.60, stitch I to H. Add, in order, J's, K, L, and M's to make pillow top.

3. Lay pillow top on a flat surface and position the basket and handle F on it. Test-fit heart D—it should extend 1" into the border.

4. Appliqué the heart, handle, and sides and top of the basket. Turn the edges under as you stitch or use freezer paper as described in "A Portrait of Hearts" (page 30). You may need to trim the ends of the handle to fit when the edges of the basket are turned under.

5. Sew G's together in two groups of five to make fans. Turn under straight edges and appliqué to two top corners. Trim pillow corners to match curve of appliqués.

6. Embellish with ribbons: I cut the ⅛" ribbon into twenty-three 5" lengths, formed these into bows, and tacked them to the basket handle. I cut the ⅝" ribbon in half, formed two bows, and tacked each to the base of a corner fan. I formed the 1½" ribbon into a flat bow and tacked it at the base of the heart, adding a rose on top.

7. Transfer the bow quilting pattern to each corner above the basket. Place the pillow top on the Thermolam fleece and quilt the bows. The rest of the design is outline quilted.

8. Place pillow front and back together, right sides facing. Stitch all around, leaving a 5" opening below the bottom bow. Clip the corners, and turn to the right side. Press the edges.

9. Topstitch through the KL and JM seams. Stuff the pillow; borders L and M will remain as flat flanges. Sew the opening closed.

# HEART POCKETS

MATERIALS:

| | |
|---|---|
| A, B, C | ⅓ yard total (can be pieced or cut as one) |
| pocket D (optional) | ¼ yard |
| lace or other trim for outer edge | 1 yard |
| ribbon for handle | ⅓ yard |
| medium weight bonded batting | 12" x 44" |
| assorted trims | |

*The heart pocket can be filled with flowers, cards, jewelry, or any other special treasure you might think of. The front of the pocket can be pieced, decorated with a second pocket, trimmed with lace, or left plain. Photos 2 7, 33, and 35; finished size, 9½" x 10".*

## ❦ Cutting and assembly:

Patterns are on page 92.

1. Cut 4 large hearts from fabric and 2 from batting. To piece the front heart, trace patterns A, B, and C, adding a ¼" seam allowance to the AB and BC seamlines (a ¼" seam allowance has already been added to the outside edges). Cut 2 A, 2 B, and 1 C. Join B's to C, then join A's to B's to make one large heart.

2. If a small front pocket is desired, cut 2 D. Place pieces together, right sides facing, and stitch along the top edge. Turn to the right side. Position on the large front heart, and stitch down the center.

3. Place large front hearts together, right sides facing, and place on batting. Stitch around the edge, leaving an opening on the side of the pocket for turning. Clip and turn. Repeat for back heart.

4. Place the two hearts together to form pocket and and hand-stitch them beginning just above the AB seam line down to the point.

5. Fold each end of the ribbon handle into a loop and tack to the sides of the pocket.

6. Add trims as desired. For my flower pocket (photo 35), I sewed on a purchased ribbon rose, tucking ribbon ribbon loops and a streamers with buttons underneath. For my notions pocket (photo 37), I tacked ribbon roses down the center of the pocket. For my stationery pocket (photo 43), I sewed a Battenberg lace doily to the bottom pocket and a French silk ribbon rose with streamers at the top. I tacked the streamers in place with tiny purchased roses.

## ❦ Screens

Several years ago, I saw an antique tabletop screen in a magazine. The picture stuck in my mind, and one day I tried making one for a friend. I employed techniques I had used previously on picture frames. My first screen had simple pockets for cards and stationary.

After my first success, my mind was in motion with new ideas. I thought of these miniature screens as portable desks, memory makers for cards and pictures, jewelry holders with billow pockets, and sewing caddies. The quilter's caddy (photo 16) is complete with an elastic ribbon for holding thread. Even though the project is mostly glued, it can have a classy look depending on the materials you choose.

The screen is constructed over a sturdy interior frame. Corrugated cardboard, heavy posterboard, illustration board, and foam core all work, though foam core is the easiest to cut. The frame is padded with thin bonded quilt batting before the fabric is added. Usually, I have scraps of batting left over from quilts that I can use. The screen sections are joined by ribbon "hinges." Laces, ribbons, and cordings trim the interior as well as the edges, and ribbons glued across the corners can hold pictures. The upper edge can be cut in graceful curves.

# THE BASIC SCREEN

1. On cardboard (or foam core), measure and mark 2 pieces for each screen section (e.g., for a 3-section screen, mark 6 sections). Cut out using either a rotary cutter fitted with an old blade or an X-Acto knife, a straightedge, and a cutting mat.

2. For each piece of cardboard, cut one piece of fabric 1" larger all around.

3. For each cardboard pair, cut one piece of batting the same size as the cardboard.

4. For a pocket, fold a piece of fabric in half. Place the cardboard section over the fold, to mark the position of the pocket, and cut so raw edges extend 1" beyond cardboard sides and bottom. By varying the cardboard placement, you can make pockets straight, angled, high, or low.

5. Place front screen fabric on a flat surface, wrong side up. Center batting on top, then place cardboard on batting. The fabric should extend 1" all around.

6. Squirt Designer Tacky glue (it sets up fast) or hot glue from a glue gun in the center of one side of the cardboard about ½" from edge. Pull the fabric over the glue. Repeat on the opposite side. Make sure the fabric is taut. Repeat at top and bottom (figure 7.61).

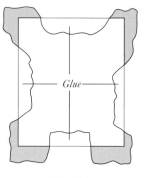

*Figure 7.61*

7. Add glue to cardboard, working toward the corners. Pull the fabric up at the corners and fold it back on itself, gluing it in place.

8. Repeat steps 5–7 for remaining screen fronts and backs (the screen backs won't have batting).

9. Add any pockets to screen fronts, gluing the excess fabric to the wrong side. Add trims to front of screen.

10. Arrange the back screen sections in order on a flat surface, wrong sides up and bottom edges even with the edge of the table. Leave ½" between screen sections. Cut 3 ribbon hinges each 1½" long and glue to top, middle, and bottom of the screen sections to join them. Let the glue dry before going any further.

11. Squirt glue around the edges of each screen section. Place the corresponding front screen on top. Hold the sections together with clothespins or pile heavy books on top until glue is set.

12. Glue trim around the edges of the screen sections.

# PORTRAIT HOLDER

*The portrait holder is a great way to display your latest family photos and memorabilia. The photos tuck into the ribbons at the corners of the screen, making it easy to rotate your treasures. Photo 14; finished size when open, 9" x 24 ¼".*

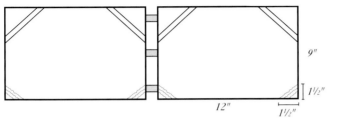

*Figure 7.62—Portrait Holder*

## ✿ Cutting and assembly:

1. Make this two-section screen following basic screen instructions steps 1–3 and 5–8.

2. Referring to figure 7.62, cut 5"–6" lengths from ribbon and place diagonally across corners. Fold excess to the back and glue in place.

3. Complete assembly, following basic screen steps 10–12.

# MEMORABILIA SCREEN

*Small Victorian cards coupled with a miniature straw hat are the focal point of this screen. Laces are used as a backdrop, and ribbons add a final romantic touch. Photo 28; finished size when open, 12" x 14".*

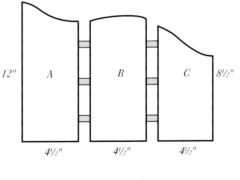

*Figure 7.63—Memorabilia Screen*

## ✿ Cutting and assembly:

Patterns are on page 85.

1. Make this three-section screen following the basic screen instructions. When you complete step 1, transfer curve patterns A, B, and C to the top of the appropriate cardboard section and trim (figure 7.63).

2. Continue assembling screen, following steps 2–3 and 5–8. Add flat trims and cards.

3. Complete assembly by following steps 10–12. Add dimensional trims and lace edging.

## MATERIALS (see figure 7.62):

| | |
|---|---|
| cardboard | 4 pieces 9" x 12" |
| front fabric | ⅓ yard |
| back fabric | ⅓ yard |
| thin batting | 12" x 18" |
| 1" ribbon for top corners, hinges | 1 yard |
| ⅜" ribbon for bottom corners | ⅔ yard |
| ⅜" flat braid for bottom corners | ⅔ yard |
| ⅛" cording for screen edge | 2⅔ yards |
| Designer Tacky glue | |

## MATERIALS:

| | |
|---|---|
| cardboard | 6 pieces 4½" x 12" |
| fabric | ½ yard |
| thin batting | 12" x 14" |
| ⅜" trim for screen edges | 2¼" |
| ⅞" ribbon for hinges | ⅓ yard |
| collection of laces, ribbons, cards to decorate the surface | |
| Designer Tacky glue | |

**MATERIALS:**

| | |
|---|---|
| cardboard | 6 pieces 7½" x 12" |
| fabric | 1 yard |
| thin batting | 12" x 24" |
| ⅛" flat trim for screen edge | 3¼ yards |
| 1¼" flat lace for top edge, pocket | 1¼ yards |
| ⅞" ribbon for pocket, hinges | 1 yard |
| ⅛" cording for pocket edges | 1 yard |
| Designer Tacky glue | |

**MATERIALS:**

| | |
|---|---|
| cardboard | 4 pieces 9⅜" x 9⅜" |
| backing fabric | ⅓ yard |
| contrasting fabric for pockets | ¼ yard |
| scraps for crazypatch | 9 different |
| thin batting | 9" x 18" |
| muslin | ⅓ yard |
| ⅞" ribbon for thread holder, hinges | 1 yard |
| ¼" elastic for thread holder | ⅓ yard |
| ½" flat braid for screen edge | 2¼ yards |
| ¼" decorative cording for pocket edges | 1¼ yards |
| ribbon roses | 4 |
| assorted ribbons, up to ⅜" wide, to trim crazypatch | 2½ yards total |
| ⅝" French ribbon for corner bow | ¼ yard |
| assorted buttons | 40 |
| felt | 9" x 12" |
| paper-backed fusible webbing | ⅔ yard |
| fiberfill | |
| Designer Tacky glue | |

# PORTABLE DESK

*This Victorian style screen complete with pockets can hold cards, stationery, and pens. It can sit on a dresser or counter. Photo 19; finished size when open, 11½" x 23½".*

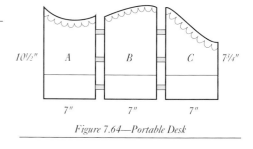

*Figure 7.64—Portable Desk*

❦ Cutting and assembly:
Patterns are on page 85.

1. Make this three-section screen following the basic screen instructions (page 70). When you complete step 1, transfer curve patterns A, B, and C to the top of the appropriate cardboard section and trim (figure 7.64).

2. Continue assembling screen, following steps 2–3.

3. To make the pockets, cut three pieces of fabric 8" x 10½". Fold in half, wrong sides together, to measure 8" x 5¼". Press. Glue ribbons and lace below the fold (see photo 19).

4. Continue assembling the screen, following steps 5–12 and adding lace trim at top edges.

# QUILTER'S CADDY

*Quilters are always organizing all their necessary tools. This quilter's caddy is complete with pockets, thread holder, needlecase, and pincushion. Photo 16; finished size when open, 9⅜" x 19".*

❦ Cutting and assembly:
Patterns are on pages 78 and 84.

Crazypatch screen (make 2):

1. Trace the crazypatch screen pattern on paper-backed fusible webbing. Label each section A, B, C, etc.

2. From muslin, cut 2 pieces 11⅜" x 11⅜". Trace the crazypatch design (reverse one) onto the muslin to act as a guide for fusing, leaving blank area at bottom.

3. Place the paper side of the marked webbing on the paper side of a second piece of webbing. Pin together in several places. Cut the webbing on the marked lines through both layers for a mirror image of every crazypatch piece—one for the right side of the caddy and one for the left. Keep A's together, B's together, etc.

4. Fuse each pair to the back of the chosen scrap of fabric. Cut around the edge, peel off the paper, and place on marked muslin pieces. When there are several pieces in place, press to muslin. Continue fusing crazypatch sections to muslin in this way. Don't worry about tiny gaps—the ribbon will cover them. When all the pieces are in place, press again. Cut 2 rectangles to fill bottom area and fuse in place.

5. Add ribbon and trims to cover fabric edges, using Tacky glue and a toothpick. Trim all the smaller interior seams first. Add new ribbons to cover the raw ends of those already placed.

6. Using crazypatch pattern, cut 4 cardboard and 2 batting on dash line and 2 backing fabric 10⅜" x 10⅜".

7. Cut two pockets 9" x 11⅜". Fold in half so the pockets measure 4½" x 11⅜" (figure 7.65). Press; set aside.

*4½" pockets*

*Figure 7.65—Quilter's caddy*

8. To make thread holder, cut an 18" length of ⅞" ribbon. Place on a flat surface. Measure 4½" from right end and mark with pin. Beginning at pin, zigzag elastic to rest of ribbon on wrong side, stretching it as you go. Working from right to left, place additional pins in elasticized ribbon to mark off sections as follows: 2", 2", 2½", 2½" (figure 7.66). You will have some ribbon left over.

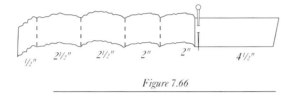

*½"  2½"  2½"  2"  2"  4½"*

*Figure 7.66*

9. Place a pocket on a flat surface. Measuring from top left edge, place pins to mark the following intervals: 1½", 1½", 1", 1". Place ribbon on pocket, matching pins, and machine-stitch through all layers at pins. Glue the free ribbon to the right half of the pocket (figure 7.67).

*1½"  1½"  1"  1"*

*5"  4"*

*Figure 7.67*

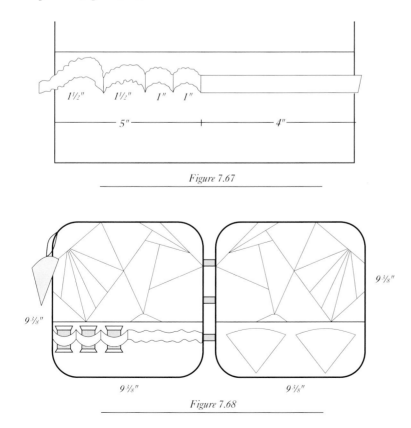

*9⅛"*

*9⅛"*

*9⅛"*

*9⅛"*

*Figure 7.68*

10. Assemble screen with pockets, following basic screen instructions steps 7–11 (page 70) and referring to figure 7.68.

Pincushion, Needlecase, Beeswax Holder:

11. Using the fan pattern, construct the 3 crazypatch fans for the pincushion, needlecase, and beeswax holder: Cut 3 each of pieces A–E from scrap fabrics and 3 of entire fan from muslin. Place A in position on muslin fan, right side up. Place B on A, right sides facing and edges matching. Stitch ¼" from raw edge. Flip B to the right side. Continue in this way to add C, D, and E. Press.

12. Cut 3 fan backings. Place backing and patchwork together, right sides facing, and stitch around the edge, leaving an opening for turning. Clip corners and turn to the right side.

13. Stuff one fan for pincushion, and stitch opening closed. Sew narrow cording around the edges, forming a small loop at center top as you go. Tack the loop and continue on around the edge. Attach pincushion to the top left screen with cording and top with a French silk ribbon bow.

14. Trim remaining two fans with cording as for pincushion. For needlecase, cut 3 felt fans, tack under a crazypatch top, and sew to large pocket. For beeswax holder, sew remaining fan to the caddy right pocket—push up each side slightly so the beeswax will fit in.

15. Glue buttons and little roses to the thread holder. Glue a button to each small fan at the top center.

## ❦ Framed Collages

*Refer to the general instructions on page 16 to create a collage with your collection. Photos 17 and 18; finished size will vary depending on frame size.*

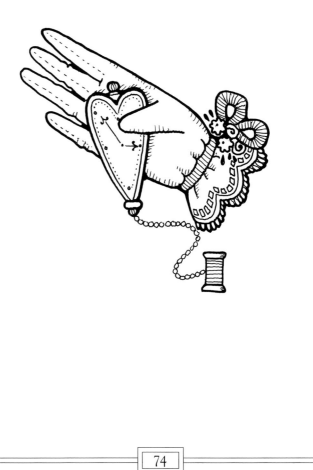

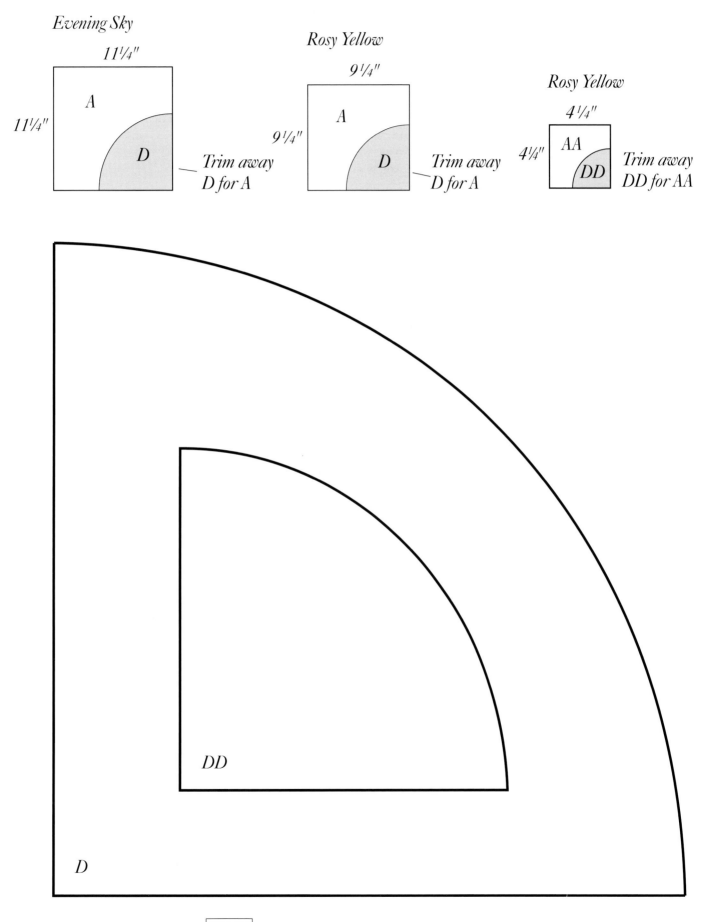

*Evening Sky*

11¼"

11¼"

A

D

Trim away
D for A

*Rosy Yellow*

9¼"

9¼"

A

D

Trim away
D for A

*Rosy Yellow*

4¼"

4¼"

AA

DD

Trim away
DD for AA

DD

D

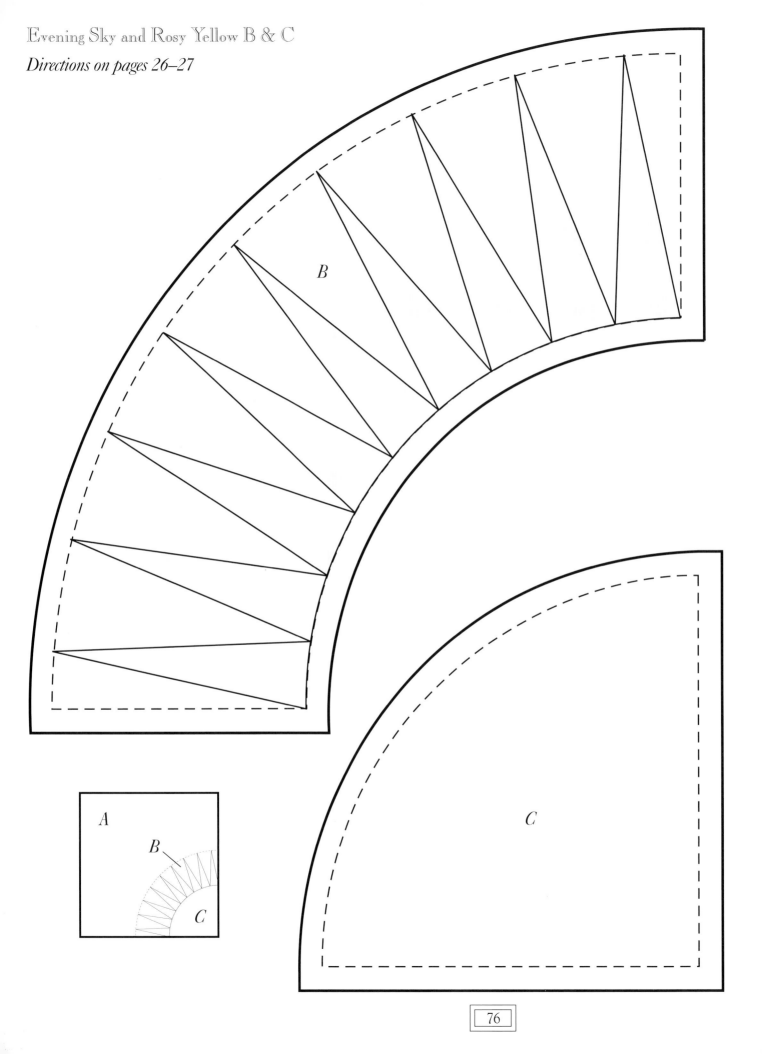

B

A

B

C

C

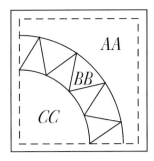

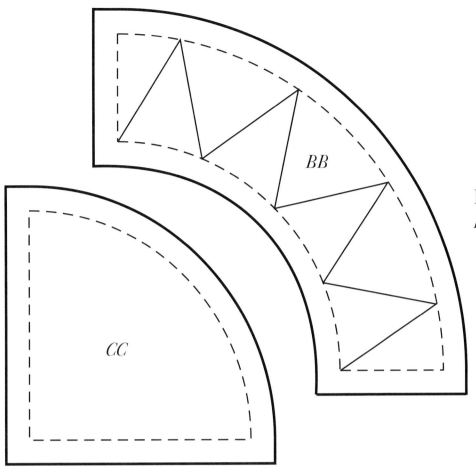

Rosy Yellow BB & CC
*Directions on pages 27–28*

Fantasy Basket Pillow and Bow

*Directions on page 68*

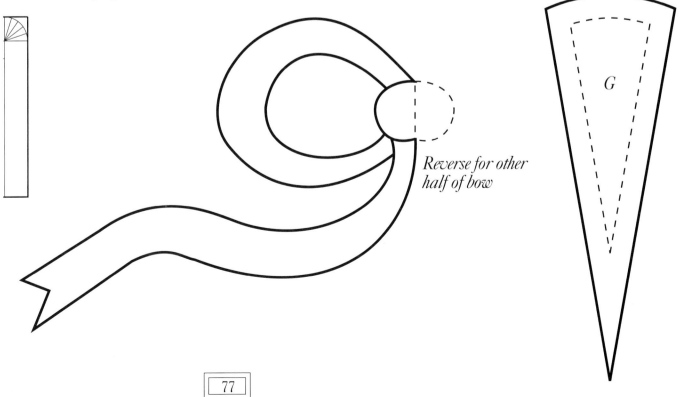

*Reverse for other half of bow*

G

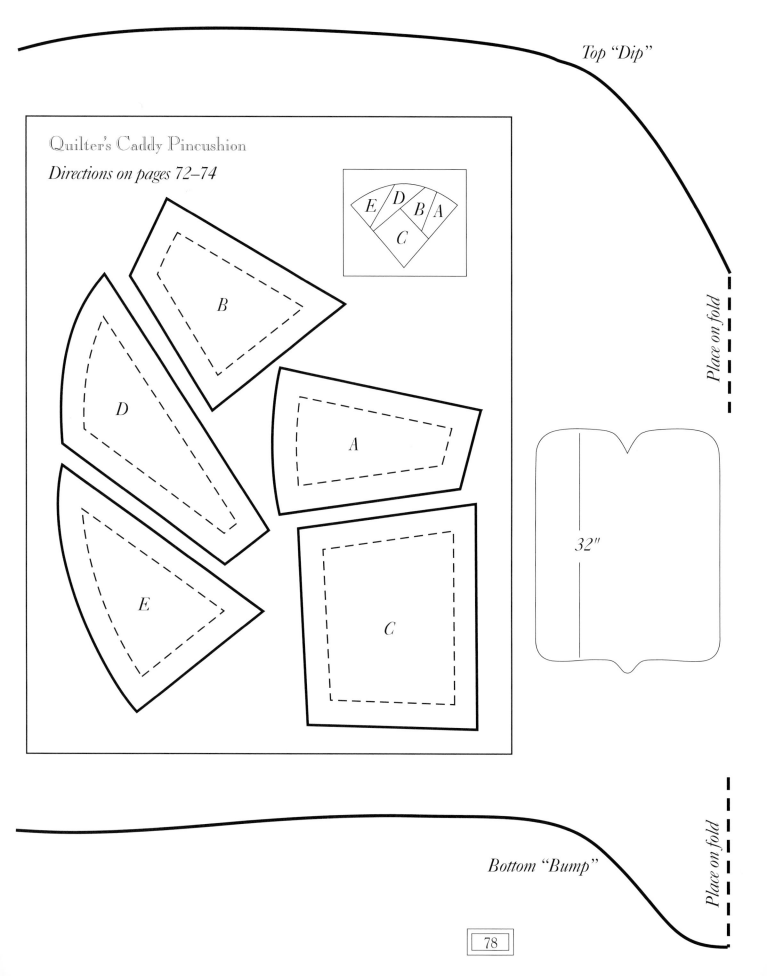

Top *"Dip"*

Quilter's Caddy Pincushion

*Directions on pages 72–74*

B

D

E

A

C

*32"*

*Place on fold*

Bottom *"Bump"*

*Place on fold*

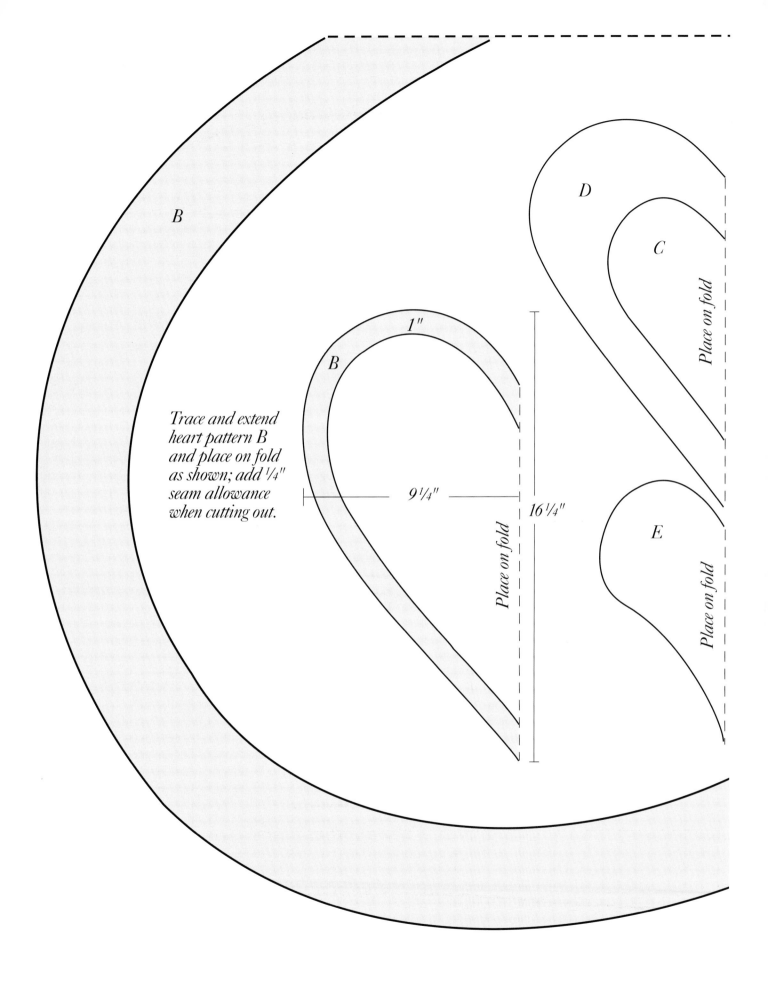

*B*

*D*

*C*

*Place on fold*

1"

*B*

*Trace and extend heart pattern B and place on fold as shown; add ¼" seam allowance when cutting out.*

9¼"

16¼"

*Place on fold*

*E*

*Place on fold*

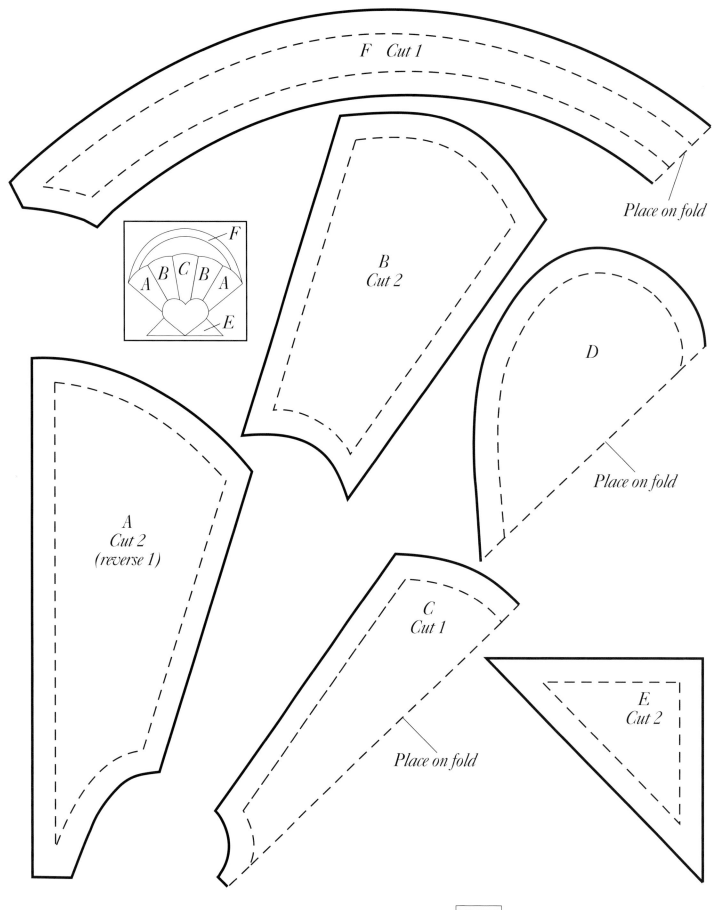

F   Cut 1

*Place on fold*

B
Cut 2

D

*Place on fold*

A
Cut 2
(reverse 1)

C
Cut 1

*Place on fold*

E
Cut 2

Cut 2 (reverse 1)

G

G

H

E

F

H
Cut 1

Four-Block Sampler
6" Heart Block

*Directions on page 33*

E
Cut 1

Place on fold

Button-Adorned Vest
Pocket Flap

*Directions on
pages 46–47*

F
Cut 2
(reverse 1)

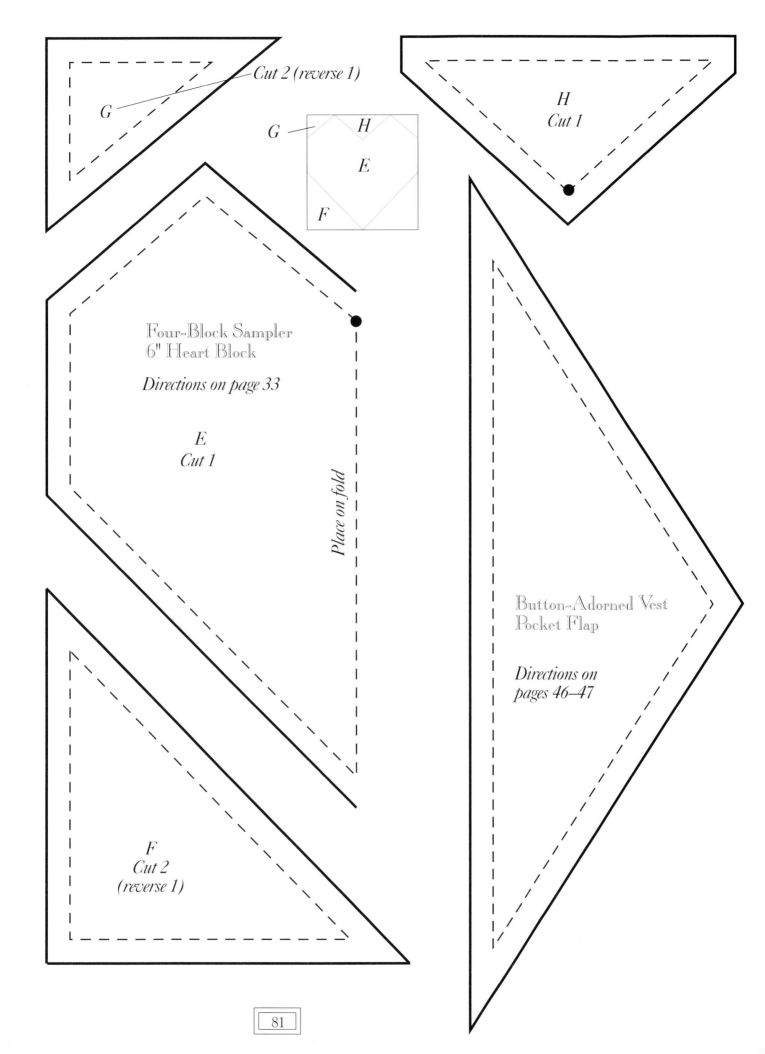

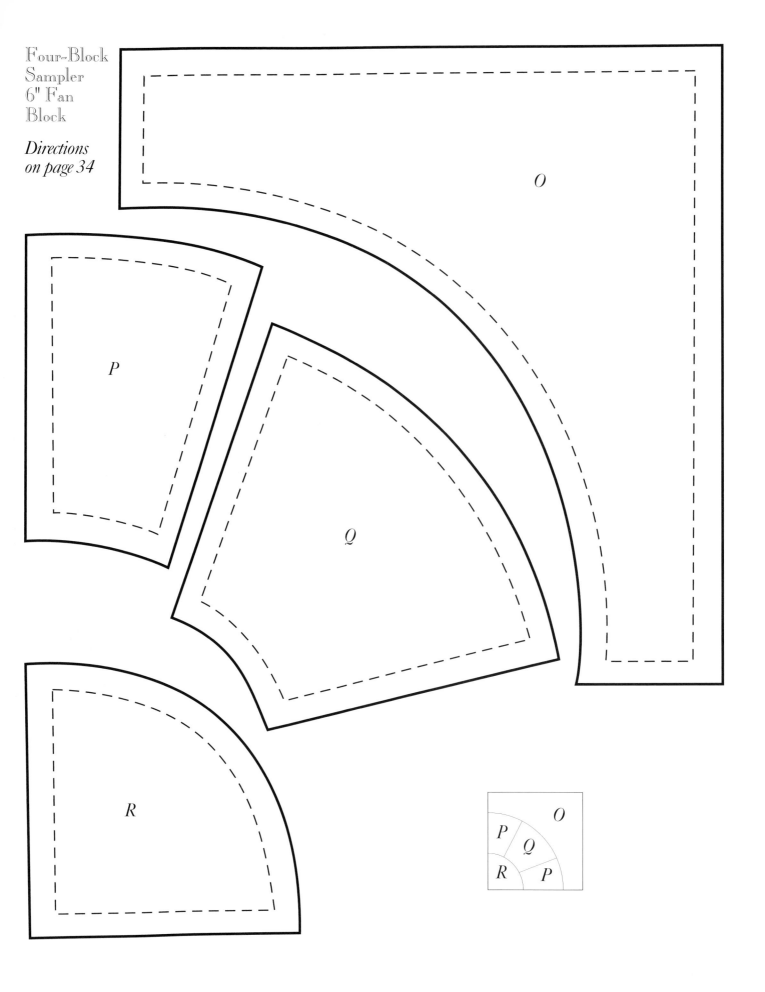

Four-Block
Sampler
6" Fan
Block

*Directions
on page 34*

O

P

Q

R

L

I

J

K

M

N

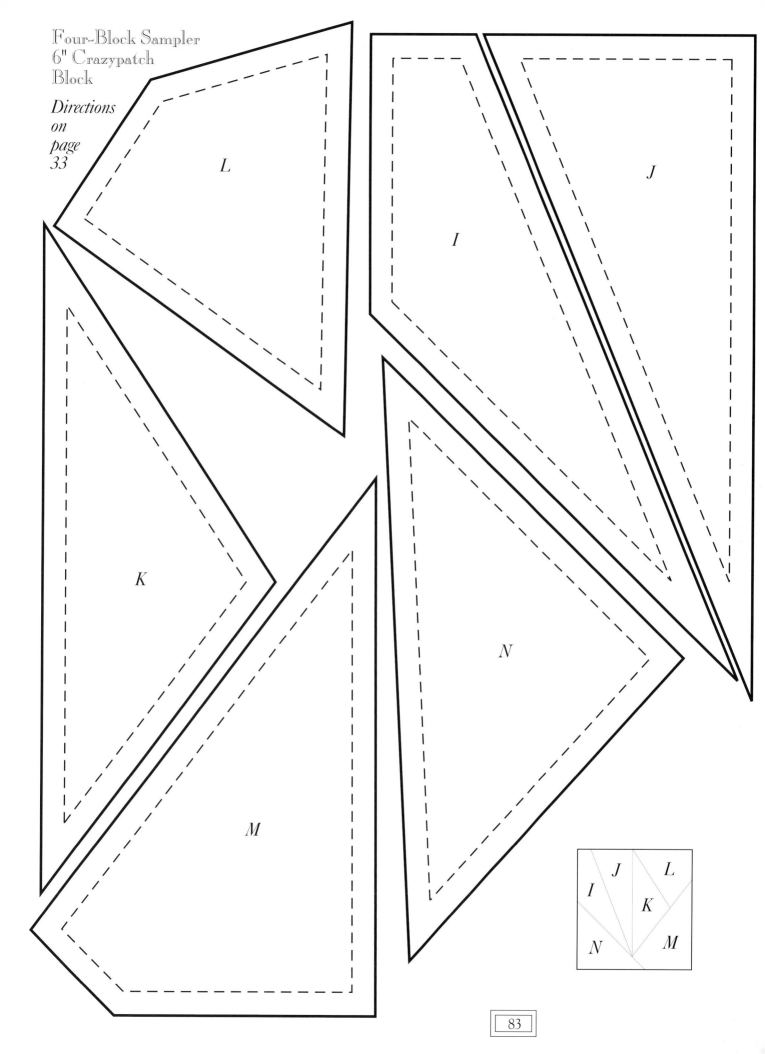

*J* *L*

*I*

*K*

*N* *M*

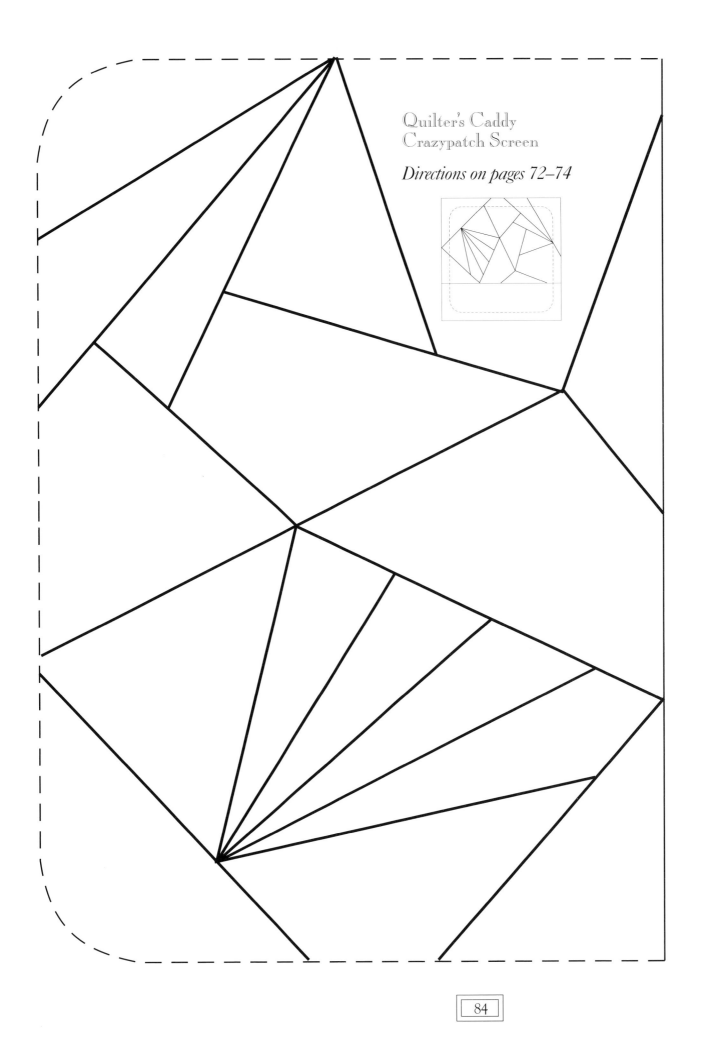

Quilter's Caddy
Crazypatch Screen

*Directions on pages 72–74*

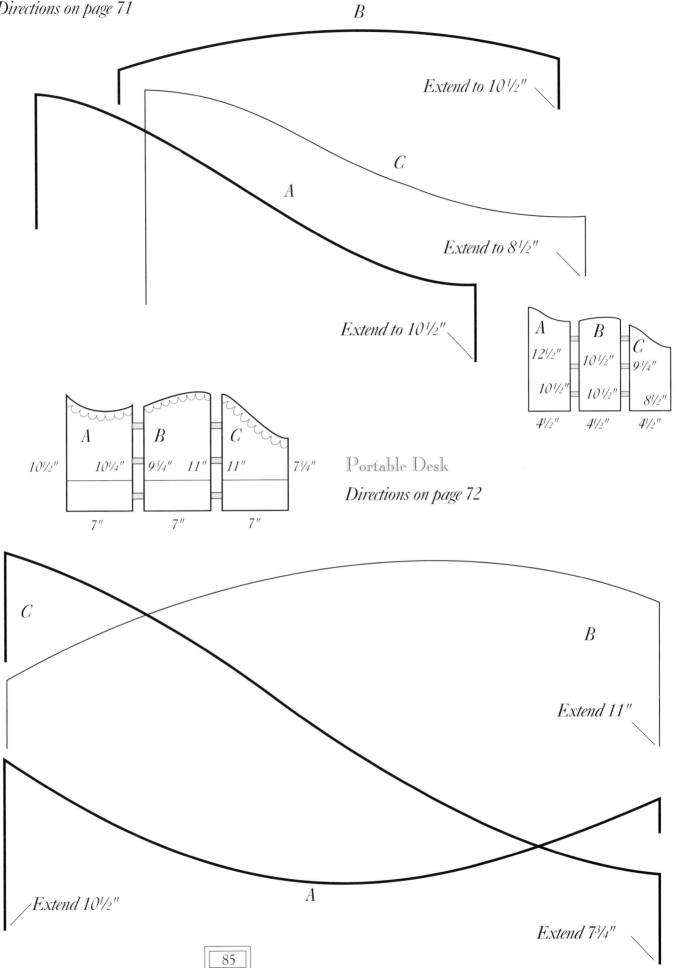

Memorabilia Screen

*Directions on page 71*

B

*Extend to 10½"*

C

A

*Extend to 8½"*

*Extend to 10½"*

| A | B | C |
|---|---|---|
| 12½" | 10½" | 9¾" |
| 10½" | 10½" | 8½" |
| 4½" | 4½" | 4½" |

| A | B | C |
|---|---|---|
| 10½"  10¼" | 9¾"  11" | 11"  7¾" |
| 7" | 7" | 7" |

Portable Desk

*Directions on page 72*

C

B

*Extend 11"*

*Extend 10½"*

A

*Extend 7¾"*

85

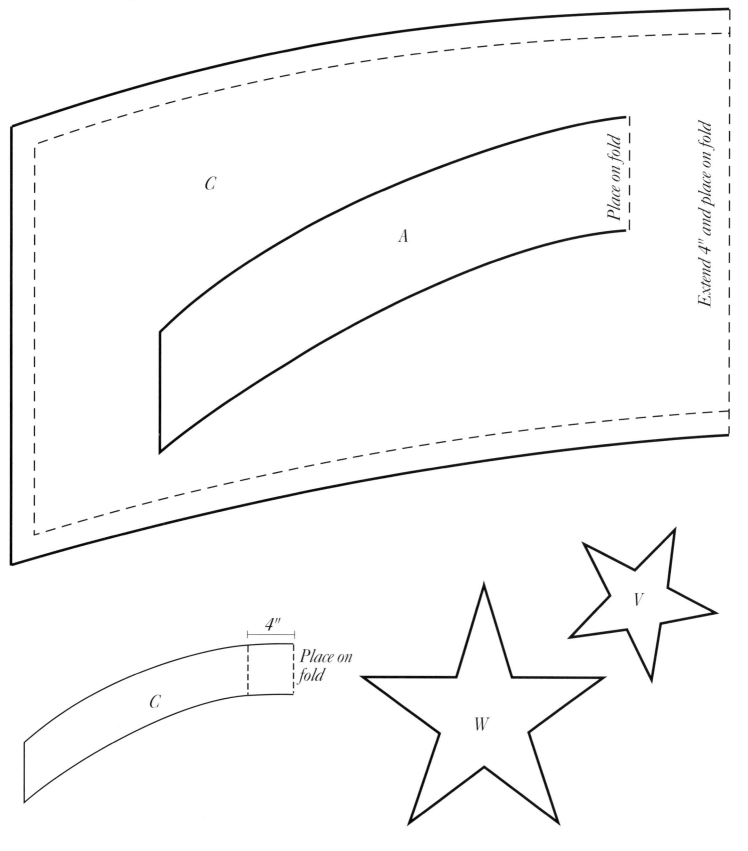

C

A

*Place on fold*

*Extend 4" and place on fold*

4"

*Place on fold*

C

V

W

*Quilting Pattern
Star X*

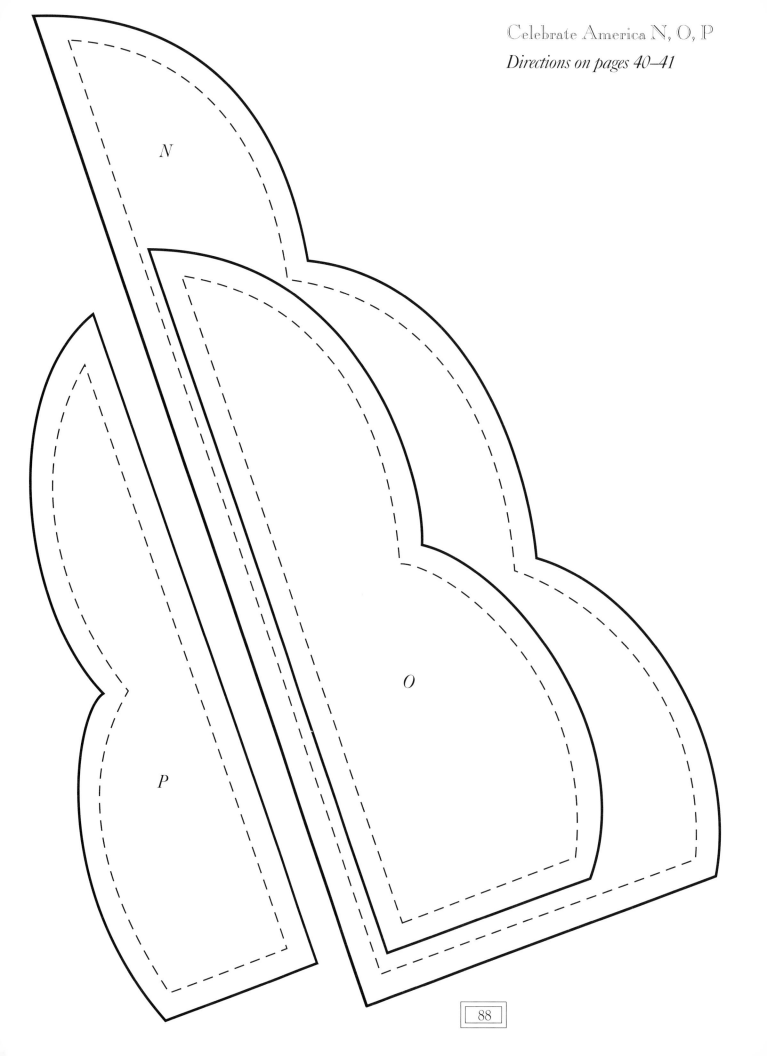

N

O

P

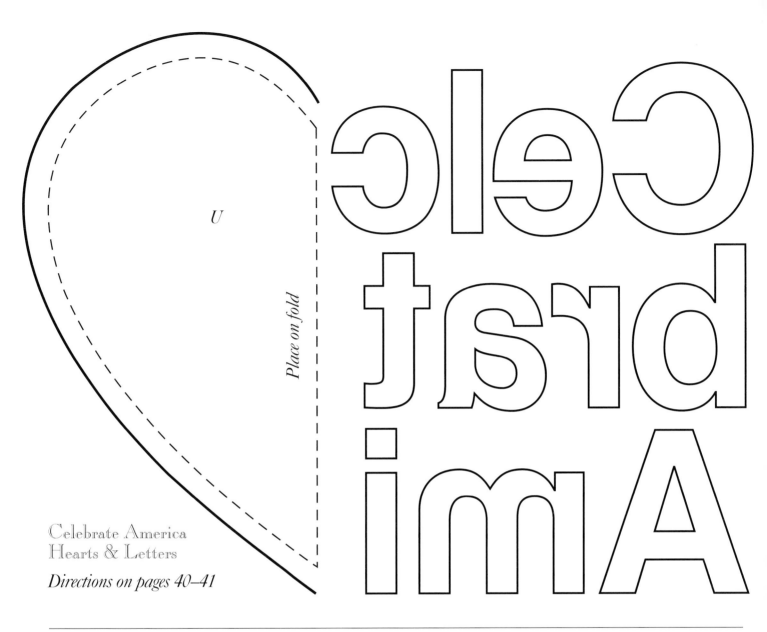

*U*

Place on fold

Celebrate America
Hearts & Letters

*Directions on pages 40–41*

---

Token of Friendship Envelope

*Directions on pages 37–38*

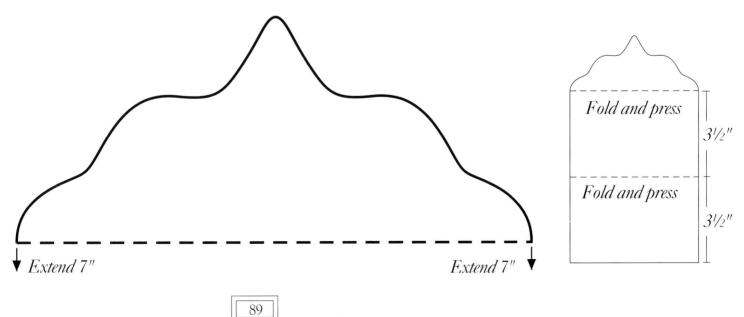

*Extend 7"*

*Extend 7"*

*Fold and press*

$3^1/_2"$

*Fold and press*

$3^1/_2"$

Token of
Friendship
Border

*Directions
on pages
37–38*

R

Q

P

O

Quilted Lace
Handbag
*Enlarge 131%*

*Directions on
pages 16 and 48*

90

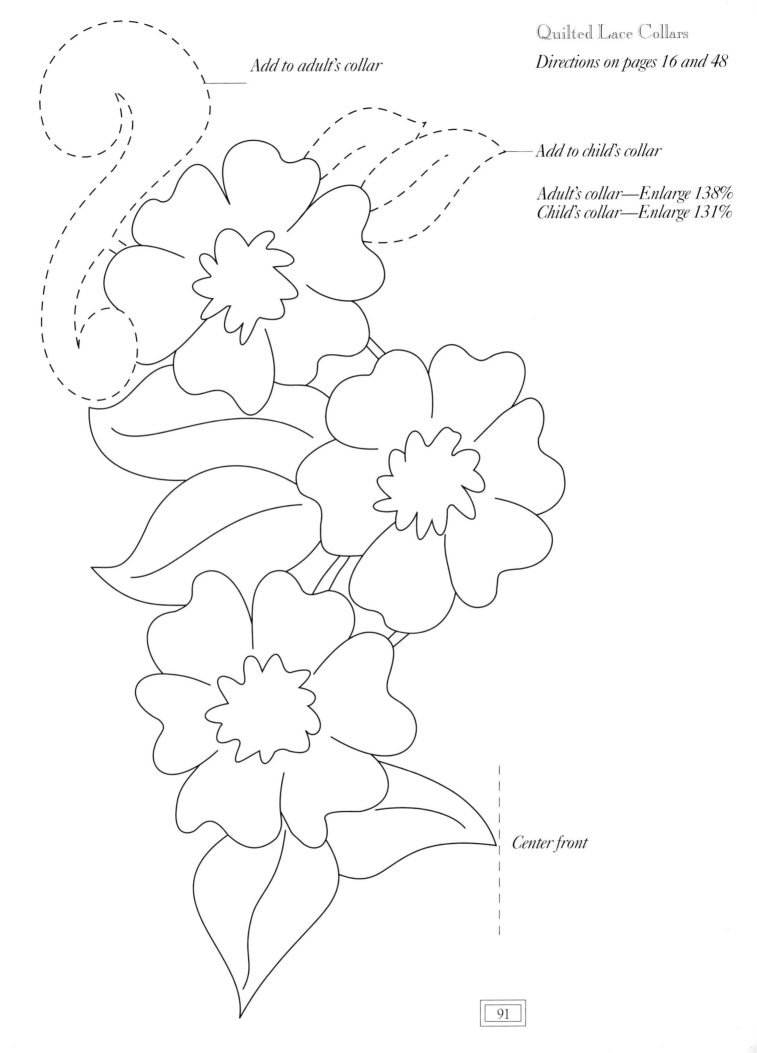

Add to adult's collar

Add to child's collar

Adult's collar—Enlarge 138%
Child's collar—Enlarge 131%

Center front

Heart Pockets

*Directions on page 69*

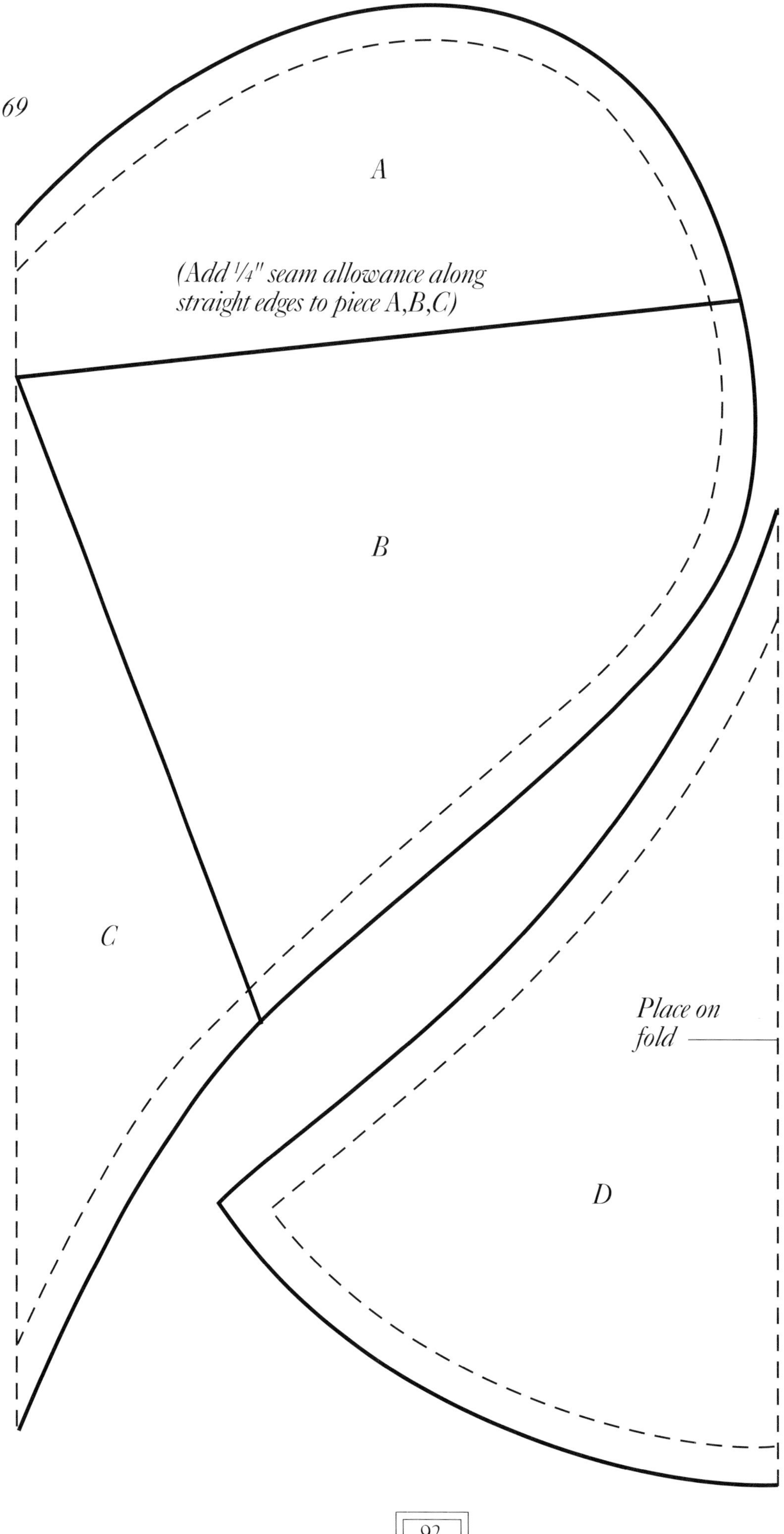

A

*(Add ¼" seam allowance along straight edges to piece A,B,C)*

Heart Button Collection

*Directions on pages 28–29*

*Template EG*
*(Reverse for DF)*

B

C

D

Place on
fold ——

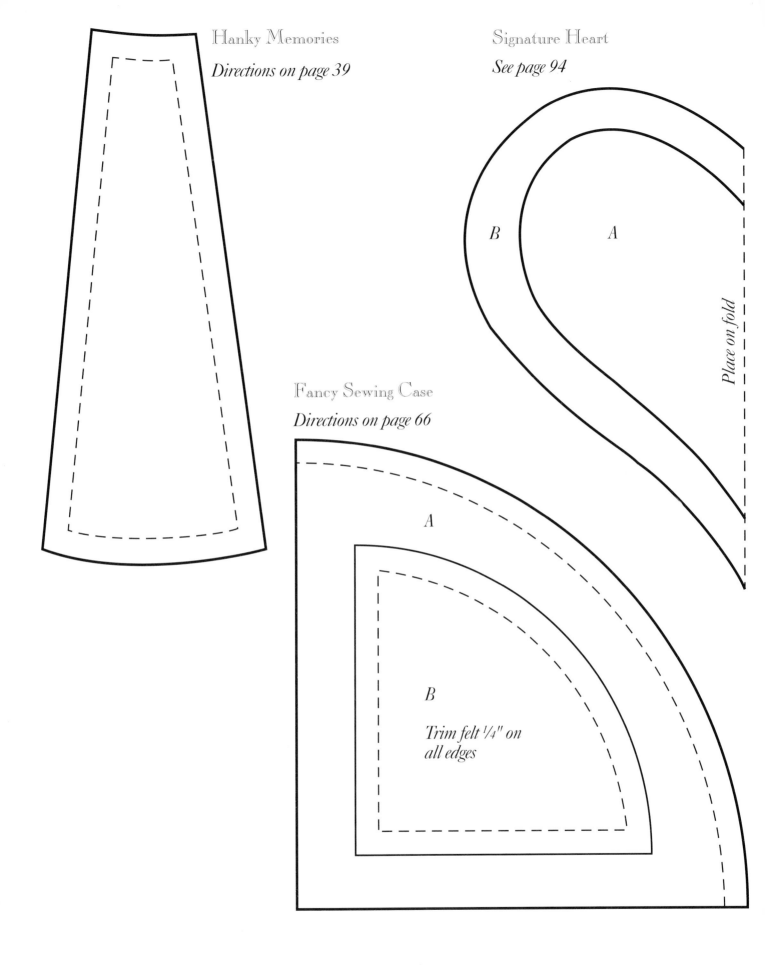

Hanky Memories

*Directions on page 39*

Signature Heart

*See page 94*

B     A

*Place on fold*

Fancy Sewing Case

*Directions on page 66*

A

B

*Trim felt ¼" on
all edges*

# Signature & Sentiments— An Epilogue

I SAVED MY SIGNATURE hearts for last. The heart is one of my favorite motifs, as you know from this book and *A Celebration of Hearts*. When I want to try out a new embellishment idea or piecing technique, I often go back to the heart shape. The finished hearts end up stuffed and become gifts for friends or little treasures for me. By adding a ribbon loop or handle at the top, I can hang them on a wall. Sometimes I partially fill them with scented flowers to freshen a room. You will see them scattered throughout the photographs. I have a hard time parting with some of them.

My signature heart patterns are on page 93. No specific instructions are necessary—just try out some of the lace, ribbon, and button techniques, or do some curved piecing or crazypatch. Experiment. This exercise is a way for you to put together some ideas of your own. Sprinkle some of your ideas with mine to create your own signature hearts.

As I finish writing *Memorabilia Quilting*, a part of me doesn't want to stop. I love what I do, and I hope my sharing of projects and techniques reflects this. The revival of quilting has become a wonderful medium for creativity in the past twenty years. I've seen women who were never strong in self-expression open up through quilting. Quilting friendships are strong and enduring.

Every quilt has memories pressed into its making, but a memorabilia quilt tells a more detailed story about the life and times of its maker. As I reflect on my own quilts, I recognize the romantic quality they carry—my love of pretty things, flowers, ribbons, little treasures. The other quilt contributors featured in this book bring their own messages and meanings to quiltmaking. Our collections always reflect our deepest memories and sentiments.

My ultimate gift to you is sharing those ideas and discoveries that have brought hours of pleasure to me. Enjoy!

> QUILTMAKING IS A PROCESS THAT GOES ON WITHIN US, SOMETIMES TAKING ITS TIME TO EMERGE. LET YOUR ENERGIES AND TALENTS RESPOND TO WHAT IS INSIDE OF YOU.

# Sources: Where to Find It

OVER THE YEARS, I've had the opportunity to try many craft and sewing products. The specific products mentioned in this book have worked well for me, but there are many others on the market you may find equally as satisfying to use. The brands listed below can be found at most sewing, quilt, and craft shops.

*Aleene's, Division of Artis, Inc. (Tacky Glue, Fusible Web)*
*Creative Beginnings (charms)*
*Elsie's Exquisiques (silk ribbons, premade flowers)*
*Emanuel Roth (lace, lace appliqués)*
*Fairfield Processing Corporation (Poly-Fil batting, fiberfill)*
*Gick Publishing (beads, charms, rhinestones)*
*Heat 'n Bond (fusible webbing)*
*Offray (ribbons)*
*Peking Handicraft (ready-made Battenberg laces and doilies)*
*St. Louis Trimming*

**Preprinted Arc Patterns** (see pages 75–77)
You can purchase the same preprinted paper arc patterns my students use to make "Evening Sky" and "Rosy Yellow." The patterns will save you the time of drafting you own. To order a complete set—10 large arcs and 24 small arcs (enough for both quilts)— send $2.50 plus $1.00 postage/handling to The Stitching Post, P.O. Box 280, Sisters, OR 97759.

**A Word about Batting**
Through my quilting and sewing experience, I have found certain battings to work better than others. For wall hangings that lie flat, I recommend Poly-Fil Cotton Classic or Traditional Needle-Punched batting. For larger bed quilts that will be machine-quilted, I like Poly-Fil Low-Loft batting. The quilt will be soft and pliable when finished. My favorite for hand quilting is Cotton Classic. You will find that quilts with a lot of memorabilia need a firm batting like the ones I mentioned above for wall hangings.

# Bibliography

Hargrave, Harriet.
*Heirloom Machine Quilting,*
completely revised and expanded.
Lafayette, Cal.:
C & T Publishing, 1990.

McKelvey, Susan.
*Friendship's Offering.*
Lafayette, Cal.:
C & T Publishing, 1989.

Montano, Judith.
*The Crazy Quilt Handbook.*
Lafayette, Cal.:
C & T Publishing, 1986.

Montano, Judith.
*Crazy Quilt Odyssey.*
Martinez, Cal.:
C & T Publishing, 1991.

Sienkiewicz, Elly.
*Baltimore Beauties, Vol. I.*
Lafayette, Cal.:
C & T Publishing, 1988.

Wells, Jean.
*Fans.*
Lafayette, Cal.:
C & T Publishing, 1986.

Wells, Jean, and
Marina Anderson.
*A Celebration of Hearts.*
Lafayette, Cal.:
C & T Publishing, 1988.

Wells, Jean, and
Marina Anderson.
*Picture This.*
Lafayette, Cal.:
C & T Publishing, 1990.

# About the Author

Jean Wells' fascination with fabrics and stitching started many years ago and resulted in The Stitchin' Post, a successful retail store of seventeen years located in the small mountain community of Sisters, Oregon. Her teaching career began in the junior high classroom and has evolved to quilting on a local level as well as the national circuit. She serves as a board member for Central Oregon Economic Development, State of Oregon Small Business Management, and Quilt Market and devotes her time and expertise as an instructor for small business development classes.

Over the years, Jean has shared her ideas through five quilting books, patterns for McCalls, leaflets for Leisure Arts, free-lance designing for Offray Ribbons and Fabric Traditions, and magazine articles. Her personal approach continues to captivate her readers, her students, and her customers.

## ALSO BY JEAN WELLS:

*A Celebration of Hearts* (with Marina Anderson)
*Fans*
*The Milky Way Quilt**
*The Nine-Patch Quilt**
*Picture This* (with Marina Anderson)
*The Pinwheel Quilt**
*The Stars & Hearts Quilt**

*From the Patchwork Quilts Made Easy series

For more information, write for a free catalog:
C & T Publishing
P.O. Box 1456
Lafayette, CA 94549
(1-800-284-1114)